GRIT
TO GO

D1568553

Published by SDE Professional Development Resources
10 Sharon Road, PO Box 500
Peterborough, NH 03458
1-800-321-0401
www.SDE.com/crystalsprings

ISBN: 978-63133-074-2

Book design: Eva Ruutopõld
Line Art: Lizzart Design

Printed in the United States of America
20 19 18 17 16 1 2 3 4 5

GRIT TO GO

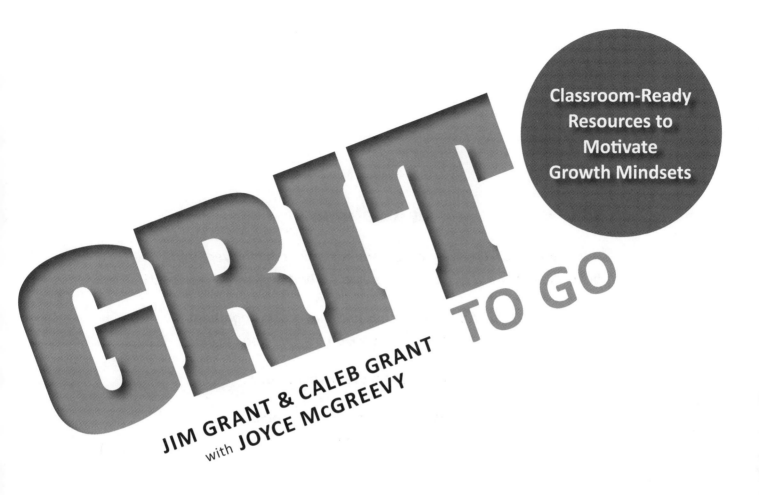

Classroom-Ready Resources to Motivate Growth Mindsets

JIM GRANT & CALEB GRANT
with JOYCE McGREEVY

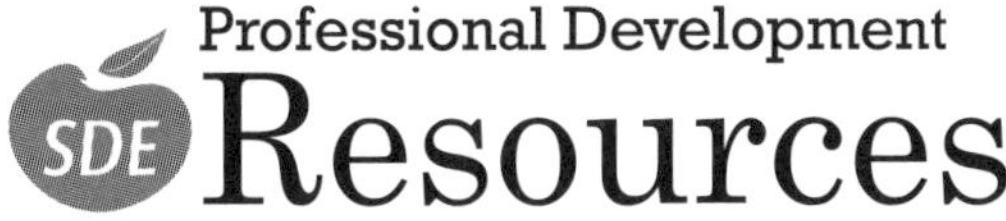

Peterborough, New Hampshire

Dedications

To my wife, Lillian, my greatest supporter who has never stopped believing in our mission to make schools a better place for kids. –J.G.

To my wife, Annelise, for her patience, encouragement, and willingness to free me up to work on my first book project. –C.G.

To lifelong learners everywhere. –J.M.

Education is not the filling of a pail,
but the kindling of a flame. –W.B. Yeats

Table of Contents

Part I: Grit, Mindset, and Motivation 1

Chapter 1: Getting to Grips with Grit 3
Grit in Action
Understanding Grit
Why Is Grit Important?
De-emphasizing "the S Word"
Grit, Meet Mindset
Why Not All Effort Is Equal

Chapter 2: Motivating Young Learners 10
The Importance of a Growth Mindset
Sharing the Science
The Power of Plasticity
Why It's the Thought that Counts

Chapter 3: Grit Goes to School 15
Creating the "Gritty" Classroom
You Are the Decisive Element
The Look of Learning
Sound and Motion

Chapter 4: From Knowing to Growing 20
Assessing Students' Readiness—and Your Own—to Grow
Assessing Mindsets
Assessing Non-Cognitive Factors Nationally: Potential and Pitfalls
Assessment: What's Emotion Got to Do with It?
Understanding Emotional State Changes
Now that We Know, Let's Grow
Honoring Mistakes as Part of the Learning Process
Are There Right Ways to Look at Mistakes?

Chapter 5: Bringing It All Together 33
A Better Way to Meet "Gritty" Goals
Mental Contrasting and Growth Mindset
WOOP Up Your Learning
Growth Mindset and Grit: They're Not Just for Kids

Part II: Grit-to-Go Reproducible Resources 39

1: Meet the Mindsets 41

Resource 1: Student's Letter 42
Resource 2: Family Letter 43
Resource 3: Mindsets 44
Resource 4: Informal Growth Mindset Self-Assessment 45
Resource 5: What's in Your Mindset? 46

2: Introducing Grit 49

Resource 6: Introduce Grit Traits 50
Resource 7: Informal Grit Trait Self-Assessment 52
Resource 8: Grit Traits Poster 53
Resource 9: Grit-Trait Cards for "Gritty" Kids 55
Resource 10: Grit Through the Ages: Traditional Character Traits 59

3: My Growing Brain 61

Resource 11: Hi, I'm Your Brain! 62
Resource 12: Know Your Neurons 64
Resource 13: Are You Stuck? 66
Resource 14: What Did You Do for Your Brain This Week? 68
Resource 15: Everyone Makes Mistakes 69
Resource 16: What if I Make a Mistake? 72
Resource 17: Focus: Your Ticket to the "Train" of Thought 73

4: Grit Really Gets Me Going 75

Resource 18: Open-mindedness 76
Resource 19: Courage 78
Resource 20: Optimism 80
Resource 21: Delayed Gratification 82
Resource 22: Self-Control 84
Resource 23: Gratitude 86
Resource 24: Persistence 87
Resource 25: Resilience 89
Resource 26: Perseverance 91
Resource 27: Hard Work 93
Resource 28: Conscientiousness 95
Resource 29: Tenacity 97
Resource 30: Social Intelligence 99

Resource 31: Grit Trait of the Week 101
Resource 32: My Grit Genealogy 102
Resource 33: Star Role Models 104
Resource 34: I've Got Grit 105
Resource 35: I Go for My Goals 106
Resource 36: Optimism: Positive People in My Grit Corner 110
Resource 37: Optimism: I Practice Positive Self-Talk 111
Resource 38: My Attitude of Gratitude 112
Resource 39: I Practice Persistence 113
Resource 40: Persistence: Word Play 114
Resource 41: I Overcome Obstacles 115
Resource 42: I Bounce Back From Setbacks 116
Resource 43: Goals: Know When to Change Horses 117
Resource 44: I Can Self-Regulate 119
Resource 45: I Have Sisu 120
Resource 46: Start with the Difficult Part 121
Resource 47: What Would Your Superhero Do? 123
Resource 48: Here's My Grit Card 124
Resource 49: My Daily "Grituals" 125

5: Creatively Gritty 127

Resource 50: Grit Cloud 128
Resource 51: Daily Grit Reminder 129
Resource 52: Morning Message-Meister 130
Resource 53: Change the Story 131
Resource 54: CAN-DO Card Game 134
Resource 55: My Six-Word Slogan 139
Resource 56: Class Grit Flag 140
Resource 57: Word Art: Grit 141
Resource 58: Word Art: Fail 142
Resource 59: Make Inspirational Posters 143

6: Additional Grit Resources 145

Glossary of Quotations 146
The Good Grit Reading List 152
Notes 162

PART I

Grit, Mindset, and Motivation

CHAPTER 1

Getting to Grips with Grit

Grit in Action

Picture it:

- Students listening to an interview with a champion soccer player are surprised to hear that as a child, she was not good at sports. The speaker shares how she overcame frustration, analyzed the way she practiced, and gradually improved her performance. Afterward, students identify grit traits and how they can apply them in the classroom.
- Five students "think their way" aloud through a difficult math problem. As students listen to each other and ask for clarification, two of the students realize where their thinking has gone off track. The group agrees to tackle one more problem.
- In a school corridor, students add images, goals, character traits, examples, and comments to a large bulletin board. The board is labeled "When the road to my goal gets bumpy, here's how I keep going."
- A group of students draws on grit traits to improve hastily written homework responses. With a little guidance from the teacher, the students list ways to "relate the traits": *persevere* in rereading a text to find important details, listen to feedback with an *open mind* and express *gratitude*, be *conscientious* in proofreading and editing your writing, and so on. Later, the students assess their efforts and share how going the extra step made them feel about their writing.
- Several students compare their scientific drawings to models of a brain. Their sketches show that their brains physically react and grow each time they learn something—which includes making math mistakes.

"Learning is not attained by chance. It must be sought for with ardor and attended to with diligence."

—Abigail Adams

Welcome to the gritty classroom. What these scenarios indicate is not who has the highest IQ, who is a "math person," or some other fixed notion about student learning and intelligence. Instead, they are all examples of grit in action—students actively harnessing the power of non-cognitive factors—the "attributes, dispositions, social skills, attitudes, and intrapersonal resources, independent of intellectual ability—that high-achieving individuals draw upon to accomplish success." This summary, from *Promoting Grit, Tenacity, and Perseverance,* a 2013 report from the Office of Education Technology, shows how central non-cognitive factors have become.

Today, that bundle of factors is most often summed up in one word—**grit**. Like the acorn that becomes the mighty oak, that one little word packs a lot of meaning. What is it that allows some people to triumph over unimaginable challenges on their way to success? They possess the "stay-the-course" grit traits needed to push past obstacles, setbacks, and obstructions and keep their eyes focused on their goals. We'll return to those traits in a moment, but first, let's examine the kernel of grit itself.

As education experts have made clear, grit has emerged, not as some fad-driven exercise in branding, but as the result of numerous rigorous studies conducted by Angela Lee Duckworth, Ph.D. An American psychologist and neurobiologist with degrees from Harvard, Oxford, and the University of Pennsylvania, and a 2013 winner of a MacArthur Fellowship, Duckworth possesses credentials that might seem to be proof enough that some people are just smarter than others. But as Duckworth herself has famously pointed out, intelligence is not the ultimate predictor of who will succeed. "Grit is essential to high achievement."

Stated in everyday language: Grit is the determination to achieve short- and long-term goals, often against difficult odds.

As an undergraduate, Duckworth wondered why some "prodigiously gifted peers did not end up in the upper echelons of their field," while "peers who did not at first seem as gifted as others" often fulfilled exceptional ambitions. She began interviewing investment bankers, artists, journalists, academics, medical practitioners, and legal professionals. "Asked what quality distinguishes star performers in their respective fields, these individuals cited grit or a close synonym as often as talent." Duckworth defined grit as "perseverance and passion for long-term goals." While her definition promotes a focus on planning for the future, we have expanded on this definition to include short-term goals as well. Including short-term goals helps reinforce the causal link between a learner's everyday actions and cumulative or eventual results. Thus, grit is the determination to achieve short- and long-term goals, often against difficult odds.

Over time, Duckworth developed the Grit Scale. Respondents would rate themselves on 8 to 12 statements, for example: "I have overcome setbacks to conquer an important challenge." We'll have much more to say about grit scales, including informal grit trait self-assessments that you can use in the classroom. (Duckworth developed both adult and children's versions.) For now let's look at how Duckworth applied her self-assessment tool.

Using this 8- or 12-item scale, Duckworth conducted a series of studies on West Point cadets, national spelling bee contestants, novice teachers in challenging school environments, and others. The most widely touted outcome of the studies was that grit proved measurably more predictive of success than IQ. That's right. Even though the responses were self-reported, Duckworth and her fellow researchers discovered that a grit score is highly predictive of achievement in the face of life's challenges.

Understanding Grit

Since that time, grit has received a tremendous amount of coverage, both in academic communities and in the popular media. Because the term grit is short and easy to remember, it's also, unfortunately, been all too easy to misapply. Athletes who might once have been described as having "heart" or "spirit" are now more commonly said to have "grit." Business people are often profiled as having "grit," in the sense of demonstrating "toughness." If the concept of grit can be stretched to mean everything from "heart" to "toughness," then it's no wonder that Duckworth's far more rigorous definition has sometimes been lost in translation.

For this reason, the **Informal Grit Trait Self-Assessment** (Resource 7) should prove helpful. Keeping this highly clarifying list where you and your fellow educators, as well as parents and students, can see it. It's an effective way to keep everyone on the same page about what is—and isn't—grit.

Why Is Grit Important?

For readers of this book, another result of Duckworth's studies that merits special attention is what might be called the "use it, or lose it" factor. In her study of West Point cadets, Duckworth was surprised to observe that being "good at things" did not correlate to students investing more time into them, even though, as she pointed out, if you were such a person, you would be "getting more return on your investment per hour than someone who's struggling. If every time you practice piano you improve a lot, wouldn't you be more likely to practice a lot?" Only, as she discovered, that wasn't the approach that many of the survey subjects were taking.

As Duckworth elaborated in a 2013 interview, "It's a similar thing with grit and talent. In terms of academics, if you're just trying to get an *A* or an *A*–, just trying to make it to some threshold, and you're a really talented kid, you may do your homework in a few minutes, whereas other kids might take much longer. You get to a certain level of proficiency, and then you stop. So you actually work less hard."

In other words, students who bank everything on being smart may, ironically, get only so far in their learning journeys. On the other hand, students who see themselves as not smart enough often feel stuck after just a few, halting steps.

Grit, however, offers *all* students the traction to continually move beyond limits. Grit traits become good habits that enable students to persist in the face of adversity, setbacks, and disappointments when pursuing their goals in school and out.

De-emphasizing "the S Word"

But wait, isn't reminding students how smart they are a helpful reminder of just how much they can accomplish when they put their minds to it? Not really, says James Hamblin, MD, and senior editor for *The Atlantic* magazine. He has written extensively about the impact of "the S word." As Hamblin summarizes the issue, "At whatever age smart people develop the idea that they are smart, they also tend to develop vulnerability around relinquishing that label."

Stanford University professor Carol Dweck knows just how that feels. When she was in sixth grade, her teacher seated students in the classroom and also doled out privileges according to their IQ. "She let it be known that IQ for her was the ultimate measure of your intelligence and your character," Dweck recalled in an interview. "So the students who had the best seats were always scared of taking another test and not being at the top anymore . . . It was an uncomfortable thing because you were only as good as your last test score. I think it had just as negative an effect on the kids at the top [as those at the bottom] who were defining themselves in those terms."

Becoming too invested in the idea of themselves as smart can make students risk-averse, unwilling to challenge themselves. The cost of any wrong answer becomes too high. The other side of the coin is to label oneself as not smart, such as "I'm not smart when it comes to (math, writing, speaking in front of a class . . ."). This, too, is a motivation killer. In either case, students lock themselves into a fixed notion of intelligence as identity.

So what would happen if we were to take "smart" out of the equation? That's where mindsets come in.

Grit, Meet Mindset

Like Duckworth, Dweck wanted to know why some people achieved their potential and some didn't. Just as Duckworth's investigations revealed the critical role of grit, or perseverance and tenacity, Dweck's research shed light on *why* some learners are "grittier" than others. According to Dweck's findings, much of it comes down to mindset, or the way a learner views his or her basic qualities, notably intelligence.

Over the last two decades Dweck has conducted multiple studies of school-age children in order to understand the relationship between mindset and learning. She found that students tend to view their ability to learn from either a **fixed mindset** or a **growth mindset**. Students with a fixed mindset view intelligence as a fixed trait. They may believe heredity, luck, and destiny have more to do with creating their future than effort. They tend to believe the future is something that happens to them.

"I'm smart," "I'm a talented writer," "I'm a lousy speller," and "No one in our family got the math gene" are all statements that are reflective of a fixed mindset.

Students with a growth mindset, however, view intelligence as "a malleable quality, a potential that can be developed." Comments like "I can get better with practice," "I love playing the really challenging video games," and "I'm learning how to write more persuasively" are typical expressions of students who believe that they can cultivate their intelligence and hone their skills with regular and appropriate effort.

Many students, says Dweck, feel encouraged upon learning that the brain is a muscle that becomes stronger with use. We believe that this scientifically validated fact is fundamental to fostering a growth mindset, which, in turn, helps motivate students to adopt grit traits. Because of this, we have devoted an entire section of the classroom resources to teaching students about the basics of how the brain works and what happens to the brain as they learn. We even explore, in a kid-friendly way, why making mistakes is all part of growing a learner's brain. We want students to understand that making a mistake is a normal part of learning, not an indication of inability.

Over several decades of school visits, education conferences, and teacher interactions nationwide, we have observed that learners with a growth mindset are almost always

- optimistic,
- up for a challenge,
- able to identify their own strengths and weaknesses,
- willing to try doing things they couldn't do before, and
- known for keeping commitments.

There's one particularly striking difference between the two mindsets—the way each looks at effort. When you reread the expressions of a fixed mindset, they tend to downplay or to rule out the concept of effort. For the growth mindset, however, the role of effort is fundamental. A healthy degree of effort is always essential, sometimes even a pleasure, and is often an outward expression of an inner drive.

In her 2006 book, *Mindset: The New Psychology of Success*, Dweck recalls how, as a young researcher, she was surprised by the reactions of some young students to an array of complex games that she had brought to their classroom:

"Confronted with the hard puzzles, one ten-year-old boy pulled up his chair, rubbed his hands together, smacked his lips, and cried out, 'I love a challenge!' Another, sweating away on these puzzles, looked up with a pleased expression and said with authority, 'You know, I was hoping this would be informative!' "

While yesterday's puzzles have given way to today's multi-level video games and simulations, the essential point is still clear: What Dweck was witnessing was grit in action. Those students, she realized, understood that "human qualities, such as intellectual skills, could be cultivated through effort."

"Working hard becomes a habit, a serious kind of fun. You get self-satisfaction from pushing yourself to the limit, knowing that all that effort is going to pay off."

—Mary Lou Retton

Why Not All Effort Is Equal

It's worthwhile to pause here and consider what constitutes a healthy degree of effort and why we should value it, since it underpins so much of what is understood—and misunderstood—about becoming a gritty learner. As reflected in the research of Duckworth and Dweck, valuing effort is not about committing to unquestioning doggedness. Simply telling our students "Work harder," "Stay at it," or "Try, try again" is no more helpful than urging someone who is visibly upset to cheer up. It doesn't acknowledge the challenge, identify its source, or offer tools for responding to it.

Effort also doesn't mean doing the same things over and over again and hoping that the 10th—or the 110th—time will result in a breakthrough. To be sure, effort often involves some repetition, but repetition alone is insufficient. Only when the mind of the person making the effort is engaged and aware can breakthroughs result.

In *The Practicing Mind: Developing Focus and Discipline in Your Life*, musician Thomas Sterner recalls that as a child he did not enjoy practicing piano. "If asked why, I probably would have said that it was boring and difficult, and that I felt as if I wasn't getting any better." As an adult, he came to realize that his feelings stemmed from his lack of understanding "of the proper mechanics of practicing, of the process of picking a goal, whatever that may be, and applying a steady effort toward achieving it." He, too, comes to the conclusion that "mindset influences everything."

Developing a growth mindset changes "the deepest meaning of effort," says Dweck. Referring to the two mindsets, she explains, "In one world, effort is a bad thing. It, like failure, means you're not smart or talented. If you were, you wouldn't need effort. In the other world, effort is what makes you smart or talented . . . So it's not just that some people happen to recognize the value of challenging themselves and the importance of effort. Our research has shown that this comes directly from the growth mindset. When we teach people the growth mindset, with its focus on development, these ideas about challenge and effort follow."

When you are self-determined—seeing yourself as having the agency to change and to grow—perseverance kicks in, and perseverance in turn fosters effort. In other words, effort becomes meaningful and sustainable when learners feel motivated. This view accords with Duckworth's summary of grit as "the tendency to sustain interest in and effort toward very long-term goals."

TAKE-AWAYS: Grit and Mindsets

- Grit is the determination to achieve short- and long-term goals, often against ˉdifficult odds.
- Grit traits become good habits that enable students to persist in the face of adversity, setbacks, and disappointments when pursuing their goals in school and out.
- People with a fixed mindset view intelligence as a fixed trait. They may view effort as a negative.
- People with a growth mindset view intelligence as a malleable quality, a potential that can be developed. They view effort as essential to the process of growth.
- Developing a growth mindset promotes positive engagement with the idea of making an effort.

CHAPTER 2

Motivating Young Learners

The Importance of a Growth Mindset

So how does the busy teacher bring all of these concepts together? We suggest that mindset and grit be taught in tandem, as one concept complements the other. Think of mindset as the hand in general and grit traits as the individual fingers. We can talk about hands and fingers separately, but they function together. Indeed, a clenched fist is an apt symbol of a fixed mindset, since both prevent the grasping of anything new. But let the hand open up and its individual fingers will support it in performing an extraordinary range of functions. So, too, the individual grit traits empower students to extend the reach of their potential and to remain tenacious in the face of challenges.

"People often say that motivation doesn't last. Well, neither does bathing. That's why we recommend it daily."

—Zig Ziglar

A word about usage: We have selected 13 traits to represent grit. Different individuals and groups prefer different traits, based on their needs and preferences. Some people consider grit itself as one of their traits. We use the word *grit* to name the category of hardy traits that have the power to increase academic proficiency, as compared to traditional character traits that make us good citizens.

The good news—and the bad news—is that the concepts of grit and mindset are not curriculum add-ons but are already built into everything we teach. The question is *how* they are built in and to what consequence, intended or otherwise. For example, an educational system that elevates IQ over EQ (emotional intelligence) is one that reinforces a fixed mindset. Similarly, as we have learned from Duckworth's studies, if an educational system does not foster the development of grit, then even among those who appear to succeed within the system, perhaps even to be its academic stars, many will lack the tools to sustain their achievement after they have graduated and must then operate outside of the system.

By emphasizing a growth mindset and the importance of developing grit, we provide students with a scientifically tested and *self-directed* system that will serve them well in the classroom and beyond. The insights students can gain about their minds and the grit traits they learn to strengthen are thus fundamental to a curriculum, not concepts that operate apart from it. Grit and a growth mindset are highly applicable and beneficial to every subject area that one can study. Consider the group of students who persist in trying out possible solutions to a math problem; the student who makes a positive shift in attitude about revising her writing; the student who learns to self-regulate, gradually replacing disruptiveness with real attentiveness, not mere compliance; the class that sets goals prior to reading a science passage; and the students who develop the courage to contribute to a discussion.

All of this has its beginnings in the mindsets and motivations of our students. While the word *mindset* refers to a set of attitudes, and *grit* encompasses attitudes, as well, ("perseverance and passion for short- and long-term goals"), the value of deliberately exploring these concepts so that knowledge of them can become power has been proven by numerous long-term and rigorous studies in the field of neuroscience. In short, while the results of fostering a growth mindset and grit will vary for individual students, the focused applications of these concepts offer all students scientifically tested benefits, not merely a new way of speaking about learning.

Sharing the Science

We believe in sharing the science of learning directly with students. As we discussed in Chapter 1, once students discover that the brain is a muscle that can grow the more they use it—specifically, once they have an opportunity to learn, in age-appropriate ways, about the science behind growth mindset and the potential grit traits that follow from it—they become much more engaged learners. Along the way, they also make one of the most motivating discoveries of all, namely that mistakes are not only okay, but also essential to the learning process. (We'll discuss the positive potential of mistakes in Chapter 3.)

"The brain, the masterpiece of creation, is almost unknown to us." So wrote the Danish scientist Nicolas Steno in 1669. Three hundred years later, another scientist, Paul Lauterbur, shone a light on this mystery with the invention of magnetic resonance imaging (MRI). Today, seeing detailed images of the brain and brain stem seems almost ordinary—a common feature of the health segment of an evening news broadcast.

However, as neuroscience has evolved into a vast, interdisciplinary field, including psychology, biology, chemistry, and physics, what researchers have discovered about the brain and the network of sensory nerve cells called neurons has yielded tremendously exciting insights into the way we learn.

The Power of Plasticity

For most of history, the majority of scientists, including neuroscientists, firmly believed that once a person's brain had developed, it was not going to change any further. You might say, they had a fixed mindset about the issue.

Among the research that helped change that dogma were studies in the 1960s that focused on older adults who had experienced massive strokes. Findings showed that many were able to regain brain functioning, a key indicator that the brain was more malleable than had been previously postulated.

Since then, neuroscientists have proved many times over that the brain not only changes, but can also be actively transformed. The brain has *plasticity*, the ability to make measurable changes to its own structure and function. The cortex, or outer layer of the brain, is particularly good at modifying itself.

And here is where the science gets downright extraordinary. It isn't only environment and actions that have been shown to alter the neuronal pathways of a person's brain, but also his or her *thoughts*.

This is not some New Age whimsy. We literally shape the physical geography of our brains, say scientists, by such thought processes as what we pay attention to or ignore, what we regard negatively or positively, what we tell ourselves about our experiences, qualities, and abilities, and by all of the other ideas and information, true or untrue, that we cultivate in the mind. Think about it—and as you do, you will be forming new connections between neurons, carving out neuronal pathways, and changing your brain.

Among the factors that influence the degree of plasticity are genetics, environment, and learning. Genetically, human beings obviously vary, yet we are all born with roughly the same number of neurons (100 billion) and synapses (2,500, which grow to an astounding 15,000 by age three). Genetics is a differentiator, but it isn't destiny.

As for environment, our own experiences as educators suffice to confirm that a child's environment has a major impact on his or her cognitive development and mindset. An environment that is safe, loving, healthy, economically sustainable, and visually, linguistically, and culturally rich is one that all children deserve, but that's not what all children experience. This in turn underscores the pivotal role of the classroom environment. Teachers who create welcoming, imaginative, nurturing, and organized classrooms (often outside of work hours and at their own expense) are not merely "setting up" a space but designing a vital environment that can positively impact the developing brains of their students, and in ways that can benefit them for a lifetime. (We'll talk more about creating the "gritty" classroom in Chapter 3.)

And then there is learning. This is the most powerful factor of all in brain development because it offers learners ultimate control—the ability to accelerate, enrich, and sustain the growth of their own minds.

It is a fact, for instance, that as one becomes expert in a particular skill, the area of the brain that uses that skill will literally grow larger. A famous example of this was reported in a 2006 study of London taxi drivers. (Maguire, Woollett, Spiers) These taxi drivers, who were able to navigate the sprawling metropolis of London by memory (as assessed in a rigorous test called "The Knowledge"), each developed a larger hippocampus, or posterior region of the brain, compared to other drivers.

Likewise, acquiring a second language, playing a musical instrument, and other extended learning experiences over time trigger changes in the brain's structure. Those changes are so specific that an expert neuroscientist looking at brain images would have sufficient evidence to distinguish the bilingual speaker from the monolingual, and the professional musician from the nonprofessional or amateur musician.

Why It's the Thought that Counts

Throughout this process of learning and skill development, we are continually thinking. What we think—the messages we tell ourselves—not only shape our brains, they also shape our beliefs and, therefore, our decisions about learning. Albert Einstein made his share of math mistakes, some of them long after his ground-breaking theory of relativity had been published. We can be reasonably certain, however, that he never told himself, "I'm no good at math."

Likewise, a person who is open to learning languages isn't going to tell herself on the first day of class, "But I don't know a word of Spanish, so what's the use?" Instead, she sends her brain messages like, "If I practice every day, I'm sure I can get this." Then when she misses some vocabulary on a test or hesitates during a dialogue, she's likely to think, "I'll improve if I review that chapter again," not "I knew I couldn't do it."

You've probably come across biographies in which people who became experts in their field encountered others who said they lacked all ability for it. Thomas Edison,

Enrico Caruso, Lucille Ball, Vince Lombardi, and most successful authors are examples. So why did they succeed anyway? Because what others thought of their ability mattered far less than *what they themselves thought*. As Pablo Picasso once said, "I am always doing that which I cannot do, in order that I may learn how to do it."

To bring this back to the classroom, remember that all learning begins with the student's belief that she or he has the ability to learn in the first place. If you think you can't, you etch that message into your brain, and your brain cooperates. If you think you can, it does the same thing, but with happier results. Mindset is intrinsic to the process, and a growth mindset is vital to the success of the process.

"Picture your brain forming new connections as you meet the challenge and learn. Keep on going."

—Carol Dweck

TAKE-AWAYS: Motivating Minds

- Growth mindset and grit should be taught in tandem, as one concept complements the other.
- Share the science. When students discover that the brain is a muscle that grows the more they use it, they become more engaged learners.
- The brain has plasticity, the ability to make measurable changes to its own structure and function.
- A student's environment, actions, and thoughts can measurably affect the growth of his or her brain.
- Fostering a growth mindset is essential to developing a student's potential.

CHAPTER 3

Grit Goes to School

Creating the "Gritty" Classroom

Creating a caring environment where students can push themselves, learn from their mistakes, and learn how to learn is essential to fostering grit and a growth mindset. At first glance, this might seem self-evident. After all, our everyday creativity and common sense tell us that an enriched classroom environment activates children's curiosity and surrounds them with helpful visual reminders of grade-level themes and ideas. However, the benefits of the enriched environment go far beyond aesthetic appeal and the signposting of information. We now know that an enriched environment can affect the actual development of the brain.

"If classrooms can support positive academic mindsets and help students build effective learning strategies, then classrooms could contribute significantly to increasing students' perseverance in completing school assignments and hence to improving their academic performance."

—Camille Farrington

Studies of laboratory rats beginning in the 1960s (under Dr. Mark Rosenzweig) to more recently (under Marian Diamond, Rachel B. Speisman, and others) show that the benefits of an enriched environment range from more efficient functioning of the hippocampus to increased survival of neurons and even neurogenesis, the process by which neurons are generated from the neural stem cells and progenitor cells. Some of the most recent studies suggest that combining enriched environments with such strategies as daily exercise and time spent in nature offers benefits to brains of all ages, findings that have given new impetus to us lifelong learners!

At the same time, this is not to oversimplify the connections between what neuroscientists have discovered in the laboratory and its implications for our children. To state the blindingly obvious, learners aren't lab rats. To simply pile on more stimuli, bombard children with high-tech "educational" toys, and devise ever more academic counterparts to mazes and exercise wheels are not at all what we have in mind. Instead, we have built on discoveries about the brain's essential plasticity to advocate for a *growth mindset environment*. This is one that supports the development potential of the whole person in and beyond the classroom, and in ways that can be sustained over a lifetime.

You Are the Decisive Element

Regardless of one's teaching style, every teacher works hard to ensure that his or her classroom is safe, comfortable, and well organized. Safety, of course, is paramount. This includes emotional safety. Growth mindsets and grit traits cannot flourish in a hostile environment. Contrary to misconception, fostering gritty students is not in conflict with creating a caring environment. Students learn best when their classrooms are places where they feel safe and cared for because this, in turn, builds the relationship of trust that motivates students to accept and even welcome challenges.

This is why the most influential element in establishing a growth mindset classroom is the teacher. As educator Haim Ginott has written, "I have come to the frightening conclusion that I am the decisive element in the classroom. It's my personal approach that creates the climate. It's my daily mood that makes the weather. As a teacher, I possess tremendous power to make a child's life miserable or joyous. I can be a tool of torture or an instrument of inspiration. I can humiliate or humor, hurt or heal. In all situations, it is my response that decides whether a crisis will be escalated or de-escalated, and a child humanized or dehumanized."

For an in-depth, scientific examination of the influence teachers can have on students, listen to the podcast of *Hidden Brain* (NPR), Episode 4: "Students and Teachers." Among the topics covered by host Shankar Vedantam and the scientists he interviews are:

- Why simply finding out what you and your students have in common is important. Preliminary studies suggest this one simple intervention strategy may be effective in closing achievement gaps.
- How the positive influence of just one teacher in just one grade level may deliver an economic advantage to a student in the long run.
- How one teacher's gritty optimism in the face of illness became a student's powerful lesson in another trait, gratitude.

It's a fascinating and thought-provoking segment that's well worth the busiest teacher's time.

The Look of Learning

In addition to safety, comfort, and organization, several additional components and characteristics are essential to the "gritty" classroom.

Visuals for a Growth Mindset. Visuals should establish the primacy of a growth mindset. Students, parents, colleagues, and other visitors need to see what a growth mindset means, how it differs from a fixed mindset, and what benefit it offers. They should also see images and text that convey a basic understanding of the structure, function, and plasticity of the brain. We have provided many such visuals and texts in the Grit-to-Go Resources, found in Part II of this book.

Reading Center/Leveled Library. A reading center and/or leveled library should explore grit across a wide range of genres and content. Resilience, persistence, learning from mistakes, and other facets of grit are important elements of the human story. As students read about achievement throughout history, they also need to gain insights into the struggles and setbacks that preceded them and the traits that enabled people to persevere. For example, when students read, "Sonia Sotomayor became the first Latina Supreme Court Justice in U.S. history," they have learned something interesting. However, when they read her comment that "I have never had to face anything that could overwhelm the native optimism and stubborn perseverance I was blessed with," they have learned something insightful that they can apply to their own lives.

Likewise, fiction in which everything works out by magic is perfectly fine once in a while, but fiction in which young protagonists face realistic challenges with grit both entertains and empowers readers. So in *The Dot* by Peter H. Reynolds, we meet Vashti, who goes from a fixed mindset and frustration ("I can't draw!") to a growth mindset and experimentation ("I can draw a better dot than that . . ."). To help you grow your reading resources, we offer several categories of gritty books in the Good Grit Reading List in Part II of this book.

Speaking of mistakes, here's heartening news for all teachers who regularly communicate with parents about how their children are doing in school and are wondering how to bring mistakes into the dialogue. As part of a study at Brown and Harvard, researchers organized parents of struggling summer-school students into three random groups:

- One group received an email or text message each week with only positive information about their student.
- One group was the control group and received no messages.
- One group received an email or text message each week that suggested ways students could improve.

The outcome? When parents received messages, the students did measurably better in school. But that's just half of the story. When parents received messages that identified areas for improvement, those students *did much better still.* When students are not afraid to make mistakes, and teachers turn mistakes and growth areas into teachable moments, everyone benefits.

Gritty Texts. In many respects, grit is about sustaining an inspired and inspiring approach to one's goals. That's all the more reason to surround students with creative and motivational words and images that celebrate grit. Better yet, encourage *students* to become the curators and creators—they can display quotations, create flags and posters, and explore grit traits through personal statements, drawings, collage, and more. In Part II, you'll find a range of options for jump-starting this creative process.

Sound and Motion

As you explore what a gritty classroom looks like, be sure to also consider what a gritty classroom might *sound* like—and even *move* like.

In *What's Math Got to Do with It?* Jo Boaler contrasts visits to two different schools. In one classroom students were almost always seated in pairs and were "generally allowed to converse quietly—usually checking answers with each other—but not encouraged to have mathematical discussions." At another school, she found students congregating around the math classroom at break time, eager for the lesson to begin. She asked them what she should expect from the lesson she was about to observe. "Chaos," said one student. "Freedom," said another.

Sure enough, the classroom looked a bit chaotic—at first. For as she discovered, the shuffling of chairs, the freedom of movement, and the increased volume of students participating in discussion groups were all part of a well-organized, project-based learning approach—and it added up to better results. Compared with students from the "orderly" classroom, the students in the "noisier" classroom demonstrated greater engagement, higher scores on national tests, and—even years later—measurably greater ability to apply mathematics to real-world situations.

In a gritty classroom, the setup of seating and work surfaces should serve the sometimes messy process of learning to learn. For example, we now know that prolonged sitting poses severe health risks. Medical experts now encourage office workers, airplane passengers, and others in sedentary situations to walk, stretch, or otherwise move for three to five minutes *every hour.* This is in order to ensure that muscles can pump fresh blood and oxygen to the brain. To put it in visual terms, Rodin's iconic sculpture *The Thinker* depicts only half the story of learning. Da Vinci's famous *The Vitruvian Man* supplies the other half.

Now no one is saying that a classroom should look like a birthday party with kids caroming around the room. However, it is with very good reason that the old model in which students only *appear* to be focused—sitting still for long periods with hands folded—has given way to a more dynamic model that supports true focus. So students need to be able to quickly and easily form groups, take part in a classroom stretch, access reference materials during relevant activities without being disruptive, and so on.

Experienced teachers also understand the power of integrating some kinesthetic, vocal, and other more energetic approaches into learning. This is not to discount the necessity or satisfactions of individual, contemplative study and writing. But every teacher is familiar with the silence of a student in a flow state of rapt attention and that of a student who is stuck or disengaged. Students who are struggling in silence, trying to stay doggedly on task but not actually understanding a key concept, are not learning perseverance—they're teaching themselves a polite way to give up.

By contrast, "gritty" students can, in all likelihood, cross the room to consult a resource, think aloud, form groups, discuss meanings and applications of concepts, share mistakes and breakthroughs, offer respectful feedback, and raise any questions or problems they have. These students are using several grit traits, from open-mindedness and social intelligence to conscientiousness, courage, and persistence. These are the classrooms where students also readily learn and express ideas through singing, movement, and role play, which in turn support students in engaging more fully as individual readers, writers, and critical thinkers. Above all, they are developing their ability to engage with the new, the unfamiliar, and the challenging. The gritty classroom is helping students strengthen the traits that will allow them to persevere.

TAKE-AWAYS: Creating the Gritty Classroom

- Creating a caring environment where students can push themselves and learn from their mistakes is essential to fostering grit and a growth mindset.
- Emotional safety is a critical component of the learning environment.
- The influence of the teacher can be life changing for a student.
- The gritty classroom enriches the senses, engages the mind, and values the somewhat messy process of learning over the appearance and management of learning.

CHAPTER 4

From Knowing to Growing

Assessing Students' Readiness—and Your Own—to Grow

"Only by meeting students where they are, Can we motivate them to travel far."

—Anonymous

If there is one word that is likely to curl the lip of even the most dedicated and effective educator, it surely has to be *assessment*. The word is freighted with negative associations, ranging from implementing batteries of standardized tests to keeping up with data-recording chores so tedious and complicated that they compete with one's responsibility and desire to actually teach.

This, however, is not the kind of assessment that we have in mind. Instead, our focus is on assessing mindset and the grit traits. The idea is to gain insight into the status of everyday non-cognitive skills and attitudes in your classroom, not to tally up numbers of times and degrees to which academic output matched input. We further believe that assessment should respect individuality and that any assessment materials should function as tools, not tasks. This is all the more important because grit traits and a growth mindset are, by definition, essential tools for students, not extra tasks foisted onto students. So by assessing students' familiarity with, or use of non-cognitive traits, skills, and attitudes, we are not labeling students or consigning them to categories. Instead, we are discovering the extent to which students have had the opportunity to personally reap the benefits of such tools.

As interest grows in measuring non-cognitive traits and attitudes that impact student learning, we also agree with Angela Duckworth and other researchers that caution is needed when it comes to how those measures are applied. "Adapting and using these measures to decide whether a program is working for a school; how to promote or hire or fire teachers, principals, or staff; or how an institution can continually improve its practice and outcomes are all different from what the measures were developed for," writes Duckworth's colleague David Scott Yeager, an assistant professor of psychology at the University of Texas at Austin and Duckworth's co-author of a recent review of non-cognitive assessments.

In the review, published May 2015 in Educational Researcher, a peer-reviewed journal of the American Educational Research Association, the co-authors write, "We advise practitioners and policymakers to seek out the most valid measure for their intended purpose(s). Whenever possible, we recommend using a plurality of measurement approaches. While time and money are never as ample as would be ideal, a multi-method approach to measurement can dramatically increase reliability and validity."

To ensure such a plurality, we have offered several options in this chapter for assessing both mindset and grit. We also recommend that teachers use any such assessments to gain valuable insights into a student's learning process, rather than to make set-in-stone decisions about a student's options. Indeed, the latter would go against the very spirit and principle of encouraging and cultivating a growth mindset.

Some brief comparison to an everyday learning tool may help highlight the common-sense approach we recommend for using assessments. Virtually every teacher we know is familiar with K-W-L-H charts. Students who are about to read an informational text regularly use such charts in three ways: First, they consider and record what they KNOW (K). Then they share what they WANT TO KNOW (W). Next, motivated and ready, they read the text. Afterward, they return to the chart to show what they have LEARNED (L), as well as HOW (H) they will learn more.

Our assessments and how we apply them function in a not dissimilar way. First, we explore what students "know"—right or wrong, helpful or self-hindering—about their own abilities and attitudes. From Knowing we move on to Growing, motivating students to develop their growth mindset, that essential human quality of wanting to know. Then, we can support them in assessing *how* as well as *what* they have learned, praising their efforts and motivating them to think aloud about the ways they will continue to learn, improve, and grow.

Assessing Mindsets

Since the ability to learn is linked to what each of us *believes* about learning, assessing mindsets is a natural starting point. We recommend beginning by assessing your own mindset.

- Take the test developed by Carol Dweck, Ph.D. Visitors to Dr. Dweck's website can click their way though 16 statements to get a quick but revealing read of their beliefs about intelligence and talent. Don't let the repetitive nature of the statements faze you. By responding according to your first impulses, you will get a surprisingly clear sense of the extent to which your midset is fixed or oriented toward growth. Go to MindsetOnline.com and click on "Test your Mindset" to access Dweck's test.

- Use the tool that we have developed, the Informal Growth Mindset Self-Assessment in Resource 4.
- We have also developed a kid-friendly option that is suitable for elementary school students. See Resource 5.

Assessing Grit

The following assessment tools are intended to yield helpful insights into individual perceptions of, and approaches to, goals and challenges. The results should not be seen as set in stone, not only because of the caveats previously discussed, but also because growth mindset reminds us that personal qualities, attitudes, and abilities can change. With that in mind, here are options suitable for both teachers and learners.

- Take Angela Duckworth's grit test. You'll find it online, along with other great resources for educators, at The Duckworth Lab online: sites.sas.upenn.edu/duckworth/pages/research. Just scroll down to the menu on the right and click on "Get your grit score." Or, choose from even more options at the bottom of the page. There you will find options suitable for both teachers and students, including an 8-item Grit Scale and a Self-Control Scale. There are versions for adults and for children, offered in several languages.
- Use the Informal Grit Trait Self-Assessment (Resource 7) that we have developed.
- For an even more in-depth study of grit traits and measurement, you may wish to explore the reports and resources published by KIPP Charter Schools. Along with an annual Report Card that is well worth reading, KIPP has partnered with Duckworth and others to develop "seven highly predictive character strengths that are correlated to leading engaged, happy, and successful lives: **zest**, **grit**, **optimism**, **self-control**, **gratitude**, **social intelligence**, and **curiosity**." For more of KIPP'S insightful commentary on these traits, go to www.kipp.org/our-approach/character and scroll to "Focusing on 7 Strengths." To read the current report card, visit: www.kipp.org/view-report-card.

Assessing Non-Cognitive Factors Nationally: Potential and Pitfalls

There are exciting developments in store from the National Assessment of Educational Progress (NAEP), also known as "the Nation's Report Card." Yes, we just used *exciting* and *assessment* in the same sentence! Why? Because the NAEP, the largest nationally representative and continuing assessment of what America's students know and can do in various subject areas, is now taking on the challenge of assessing non-cognitive skills. Beginning in 2017, NAEP will use surveying to collect data on such core areas as motivation, mindset, and grit. Core areas listed in the background survey include:

- Students' non-cognitive skills: grit, desire for learning
- Non-cognitive school factors: school climate, technology use
- Home and environment factor: socioeconomic status

Press releases about the upcoming survey have noted that teachers report spending as much as 10 percent of their instructional time on non-cognitive skills. At the same time, responses from some of the very researchers who helped popularize the teaching of such skills in the first place make plain that NAEP's findings should not be used—or more to the point, misused—for a host of other accountability measures, ranging from diagnosing students for tracking or remediation to evaluating educators and comparing schools.

In an essay entitled "Measurement Matters: Assessing Personal Qualities Other than Cognitive Ability for Educational Purposes, Angela Duckworth and David Scott Yeager remind policy makers and educators that existing questionnaire measures were originally developed for research purposes. Until such measures and performance tasks have been adapted and refined through further collaboration between practitioners, researchers, program evaluators, and developers, they will be "ill-suited for accountability purposes."

Acknowledging the growing interest in the promotion of non-cognitive qualities, ranging from behaviors and beliefs to skills, Duckworth, the leading spokesperson for grit, and Yeager, a key researcher of growth mindset, comment: "We share this more expansive view of student competence and well-being, but we also believe that enthusiasm for these factors should be tempered with appreciation for the many limitations of currently available measures."

Among the limitations that must first be addressed, say Duckworth and Yeager, are

- misinterpretation, such as when respondents interpret a questionnaire item in a way that does not accord with the researcher's intent;

- insufficient detail or insight in reporting behaviors, motivations, and emotions; and
- various biases, that can result in groups of respondents applying conflicting frames of reference or consciously or unconsciously providing answers that are desirable but not accurate.

Duckworth and Yeager also present detailed steps that could help unlock the potential of non-cognitive skill measurement, including further investment into the research and development and training necessary "to yield measures and measurement practices that could empower those seeking to cultivate these important qualities in students."

The Walton Family Foundation has already announced plans to issue grants totaling $6.5 million to several groups of researchers, including Duckworth's lab at the University of Pennsylvania; the Character Lab of New York, co-founded by Duckworth, KIPP chart schools co-founder Dave Levin, and Riverdale Country School head Dominic Randolph; and Martin West, whose Boston Charter Research Collaborative works with Harvard and the Massachusetts Institute of Technology. It remains to be seen how or if researchers' focus on developing more nuanced and reliable measures, the foundation's desire to scale intervention and accountability, and critics' concerns for addressing systemic issues, ranging from curricula to socioeconomic factors can be synthesized into a shared understanding of the practices most likely to benefit students.

"Not everything that can be counted counts, and not everything that counts can be counted."

—Albert Einstein

Meanwhile, teachers continue to engage students directly, all day and every day, charged with nothing less than promoting the relevance of the learning content and the learning process; communicating concern for their students' safety, health, and well-being; convening multi-modal explorations of themes, virtues, and values; modeling character-building behavior, intellectual curiosity, critical thinking, and artistic creativity; providing the ideal balance of acceptance, validation, and challenge—and all while monitoring the individual and collective progress, setbacks, and changes of complex human beings. Piece of cake.

So with the researchers' caveats in mind, we will proceed cautiously into the issue of assessing students' emotional states.

Assessment: What's Emotion Got to Do with It?

Understanding emotional state changes is important both from a teacher's and a student's perspective. Stress and anxiety among school-age children is a source of growing concern to educators. A 2013 survey by the American Psychological Association of more than 2,000 people revealed that stress in adolescents rivals that of adults. In 2015, the WebMD Stress in Children Consumer Survey reported what many teachers already know, namely that children are showing signs of stress as early as elementary school, but their parents may not always recognize it as such. The parents surveyed did report negative physical and behavioral issues, yet a significant number did not attribute the issues to stress.

Much of this anxiety and stress can result from simply not knowing what to do when confronted with challenges, disappointments, changes, and expectations. Guiding students to develop a growth mindset helps them to become flexible in their thinking and open to learning new attitudes and behaviors. Modeling the practice of grit traits can help students respond, rather than to react, to situations they associate with stress.

In Chapter 3, we talked about creating a safe and caring classroom, and it will come as no surprise to teachers that this includes providing emotional safety that allows personal growth, with its inevitable ups and downs, to flourish. As Eric Jensen and LeAnn Nickelsen, the authors of *Deeper Learning* share, "to love learning and to have the motivation to learn deeply is a key to . . . cultivating our personal growth." To foster such motivation and build a positive learning culture, they believe, pre-assessment must also include knowing your students personally, including their emotional states. "The ideal emotional state is not a flat affect (boredom, apathy, or detachment) . . . [but] a fresh, relaxed, and alert curiosity."

We would take this one step further: Not only should our assessments help us know our students, but assessment should help students know themselves. This includes developing their metacognition, or the ability to think (often aloud) about their thinking. It also means helping students develop the vocabulary to articulate their emotions. For example, in a 2015 interview, Sandra Hassink, MD, president of the American Academy of Pediatrics pointed out that, "Younger children don't usually talk about being 'stressed' in those terms."

The student who gains insight into his or her own attitudes, traits, and emotional intelligence—who is conversant in, and able to apply, the concepts of growth mindset and grit traits—is a student who is empowered to self-regulate, develop resilience, make informed choices, grow, and ultimately to become a self-motivated, autonomous learner.

With this in mind, take a look at Understanding Emotional State Changes, a reminder of the circumstances that may impact a person's emotional state of mind (see below). See also Part II activities and reading list options that provide students with opportunities to explore and strengthen their emotional/social intelligence.

Understanding Emotional State Changes

Everyday events, one's thoughts, and other external and internal factors can trigger chemical changes in the brain that affect a student's emotions. Such emotional state changes can impact a student's behavior and attitude for better or worse.

In the latter case, modeling gritty coping skills for students can help mitigate the anxiety or fear that is almost always at the root of negative states. So it's very important to be attuned to these emotional state changes, including in ourselves. Factors include, but are not limited to:

- the environment
- the weather
- changes of season/ seasonal affective disorder
- light/ aromas/temperature
- daily diet
- hydration
- sleep
- good news/bad news/threats
- perceived threats
- physical activity
- social media
- a person in authority
- music
- family/friends

Now that We Know, Let's Grow

Setting and raising expectations is critically important to motivating a growth mindset and fostering grit. It is also often misunderstood. Fostering grit doesn't mean being "tough" on kids or pushing them to extremes, any more than "growth" means expecting all kids who take piano lessons to become concert-level virtuosos. However, even as we rightly abhor such extremes, we need to also steer clear of equally insidious extremes at the gentler end of the spectrum.

For instance, one of the surest ways to kill motivation is to accept passivity. Such passivity manifests itself in a myriad of subtle ways.

Imposed Attitudes or Excuses. "Nobody in my/that family has ever been any good at . . ." Attitudes and learning abilities may be modeled, but they are *not* inherited. Students, and for that matter the families who love them, can grow, learn, and thrive. By motivating students to develop a growth mindset and grit, we model for them how to move beyond imposed definitions of who they are and empower them to decide personal roles and goals for themselves.

Learned Helplessness. "I give up." Learned helplessness may be a habit, but it is not a permanent condition. Students can overwrite learned helplessness with new behaviors. An associate of ours vividly remembers the first time a librarian encouraged her to switch from reading 16- to 24-page picture books to reading her first chapter book. "It would take me my entire life to read all that!" she wailed. To which the librarian replied with a smile, "Start reading now and see if you still feel that way in an hour." Needless to say, our associate has since gone on to read (and write) many more books, with no adverse impact on her health.

No Free Passes. "Oh, don't worry, that's good enough. Go play." When children hear a comment like this from a parent or teacher, it may feel like a free pass, but it's really an infringement on their potential. It's also setting them up for a rude awakening in adulthood, when they're unlikely ever to hear, "Oh, don't worry about speeding. I'm sure you didn't mean it," or "Don't worry about getting that tax return in on time."

The extreme opposite of letting someone off the hook has been handed down to us through the well-known folktale, "Rumplestiltskin." "Before the dawn, you must spin a roomful of straw into gold." No one is suggesting that we give students punitive ultimatums designed to break their spirits. What we know for certain, however, based on the research of flow states, engagement, and motivation by Mihaly Csikzentmihalyi (CHICK-sent-mee-high), Michael Smith, Eric Jensen, and others, is this: Without *enough* of a challenge, students quickly become disengaged. As Joseph Smigelski wrote in an introduction to reading Shakespeare, and which is equally applicable to "learning adventures" in general, "Nothing worth having comes easily. The enjoyment kicks in when you really start to get it."

So while we would never issue draconian ultimatums to a student, we actually owe it to students to encourage them to make more of an effort. For example, we can use statements such as, "You're so close! Please keep at it just a few minutes longer,"

"I see that you're persevering and making a real effort," and "Stay focused now and let your mind come up with more ideas." In other words, meeting challenges isn't about moving a mountain in a single push, but rather about making a steady, daily effort toward the good. As blogger Sarah Peck says in an inspiring essay entitled "Show Up," "It's about the accumulation of micro-actions."

Honoring Mistakes as Part of the Learning Process

Quick—what's the difference between playing a video game and taking a standardized test? Answer: The video game almost always allows you to learn from mistakes.

Next question: What do live sports events and theatre productions have in common? Answer: After the seats empty, players gather to acknowledge their hits and misses and to focus their strategic efforts on improvement. These sessions have something else in common—they ultimately boost morale because they focus on collective, incremental growth.

In an encouraging if nascent development, groups as diverse as medical institutions and commercial airlines, technology start-ups and nonprofits are starting to appreciate the need to engage mistakes, not ignore them. After all, making mistakes is one of life's inevitabilities. As author J.K. Rowling has said, "It is impossible to live without failing at something, unless you live so cautiously that you might as well not have lived at all—in which case, you fail by default." Or as UCLA football coach John Wooden once commented, "If you're not making mistakes, then you're not doing anything. I'm positive that a doer makes mistakes."

Unfortunately, while a growing number of individuals and organizations recognizes that mistakes are potentially rich in lessons, when it comes to our kids, many of us still view mistakes as an outcome to be avoided at all costs—and the cost, it turns out, is high indeed. Ironically, it's the very fear of making mistakes, and the risk-averse behaviors that such an attitude engenders, that can keep a young learner from succeeding in the fullest sense of the word.

For instance, the student who prioritizes (or whose parents prioritize) getting high scores over and above more process-oriented learning goals is likely to avoid anything that might lower his or her scores. What is particularly insidious is that this fear of failure can be inculcated in students in seemingly contradictory ways. On the one hand, many kids are labeled as "smart" and come to fear losing what they misperceive as their core identity. On the other hand, many students are labeled as "not smart enough." Consider what happens when generations of girls grow up being told that they can't learn math and science as well as boys. As educator Jo Boaler points out, such messages make girls more likely to avoid challenging themselves in science and math, and that aversion to making mistakes leads to less learning and progress. When students believe that the only things worth learning are whatever they can "get right" on the first attempt, their realms of interest shrink dramatically.

Thus "playing it safe" actually traps students in their comfort zones and renders them ill-prepared for challenges beyond the classroom. Furthermore, the fear response to mistakes—even to the very prospect of making a mistake—interferes with a person's brain chemistry, which in turn impedes our ability to take in new information. Now imagine a classroom culture that makes it safe to stop playing it safe. That's the gritty classroom, a place where mistakes becomes stepping-stones to more effective learning and greater growth.

Are There Right Ways to Look at Mistakes?

Whether we regard failure as a catastrophe or an opportunity is a key indicator of our mindset. The ways that we as a culture educate and parent our young people sends a powerful message about how we view setbacks and disappointment. In *Freedom to Fail*, Andrew K. Miller recalls getting a mediocre score on a school test for which he was unprepared. What strikes him as particularly revealing about the experience is not the absence of quizzes leading up to the test but rather what happened *after* the test—nothing. No do-overs, no re-teaching, and by implication, no classroom discussion or think-alouds. "My failure, in this case," he says, "was treated as exclusively negative and final."

By contrast, a gritty classroom would recognize in his and other students' mistakes the beginning of a whole new learning opportunity. As scientific studies show, mistakes are essential information and as such, they are integral to learning.

- When we throw a baseball pitch too low, a special form of memory stores that away to help inform our next attempt (R. Shadmehr).
- When we make a mistake in math, it causes synapses to fire and promotes the development of our brain. (J. Boaler).
- When we challenge ourselves to come up with answers at the start of a lesson, *when there's a high probability of being incorrect*, we sharpen our critical attention to, and recall of, what we subsequently study (L. Richland, N. Kornell, L. Kao).

These are just a few examples of how mistakes play a role in learning. Making mistakes also signifies engagement, effort, and progress. Just consider the toddler who says, "We wented to the park yesterday." Reflected in that mistake is a budding awareness of grammar and the motivation to apply it. No adult would ever respond to such an endearing scenario by simply retorting, "Wrong!" Instead, we'd acknowledge the effort with a smile and act on the teachable moment.

So how do we give students the opportunity to make and learn from mistakes? Here are some suggestions.

Be Upfront. First and foremost convey the message that mistakes are part and parcel of learning. In *Freedom to Fail* (ASCD, 2015), Andrew K. Miller recommends that, "when teachers set norms for the classroom at the beginning of the year, they should also share norms related to failure with students."

Talk and Think Aloud. Students need to know, and feel safe with, a practice of regularly thinking aloud about what and how they are learning. Everything from discussing where students went astray in working on a math problem to how students share feedback during writing becomes a positive practice.

Offer Parents a Way Onboard. As a parent and a teacher, Jessica Lahey truly understands the wish to protect, even overprotect, one's children and the will to promote their independent growth. Her best-selling book, *The Gift of Failure: How the Best Parents Learn to Let Go so Their Children Can Succeed* (HarperCollins, 2015), is a goldmine of practical wisdom that parents will find highly relatable and empathetic. "The less we push our kids toward educational success, the more they will learn," she tells one mom. Lahey also acknowledges parents' worry that "even if they adopt a rosy view of failure, their child is too afraid to fail. I tell them to watch their child undertake a task they love, under their own motivation and control, and see just how afraid of failure that kid really is. A child who flips out over challenging fractions during homework time is the same child who will sit down to play Minecraft for three hours, gleefully overcoming repeated obstacles . . . ."

Elevate the Role of Questions. Under the category of "No Surprise, Sherlock," file the many studies showing that students who ask questions are less confused and more engaged than students who don't. But as educators also know, asking questions offers much more than expedient clarification, especially in light of the positive role that mistakes can play in learning. Asking questions simply to "get the answer" pales in value when compared with asking questions to become more analytical, reflective, and curious.

In the gritty classroom, students ask copious questions, including to dive deeper into a topic, examine their concepts and misconceptions of it, map areas of challenge, and problem-solve. Likewise, gritty teachers often give feedback in the form of questions, such as asking students how they came up with a certain answer, where they ran into difficulty, or identifying what steps they could take next.

Jaime Kaizal, a teacher in Arizona, reports, "After the class has decided on the 'right' answer, I will frequently ask, 'Who can share with us where you made your mistake?' Students then feel successful in their ability to pinpoint what they need to do differently next time."

Celebrate Effort. It's no wonder that effort so often goes ignored in our culture. Just look at how news reports on political campaigns increasingly focus on candidates' standings in the polls but offer few evaluations of their efforts as policymakers to improve the lives of voters. Likewise, students are sometimes victims of this winners-and-losers perspective.

To paraphrase Shakespeare, the fault is not in our gold stars, but in how our culture awards them. Consistently praising children as "gifted" or "smart" is a fixed-mindset approach. It reinforces the notion that, through fate or random chance, some people are born with the "right" traits; some people aren't; and there's not a thing that can be done about it. It can also lead students to attribute any progress or setbacks to sheer luck rather than to factors within their control.

In the gritty classroom, teachers praise the efforts that students make:

- "It's clear that you gave this all your attention. How did you go about it?"
- "You added more detail this time."
- "Well done. You are ready to practice the next step."

Far from being a consolation prize, acknowledgment of effort is a highly practical way of reinforcing the behaviors and attitudes that will best help students fulfill their potential. It also helps students recognize how essential it is to be consistent.

TAKE-AWAYS: Assessing and Challenging

- Assessment of non-cognitive skills and attitudes in your classroom is essential to encouraging a growth mindset and fostering grit.
- Since the ability to learn is linked to what each of us believes about learning, assessing mindset—including your own—is a natural starting point.
- Considering emotional states and the factors that impact them will not only benefit you as teacher, but also help students better understand and direct themselves as learners.
- Raising expectations is key to motivating learners. Students can evolve beyond learned helplessness and other forms of disengagement.

"I was lucky to be brought up by parents who pushed me to try new things and who allowed me to make mistakes. When I did make a mistake, sometimes they reached down a hand, and sometimes they said, 'We know that you can figure it out yourself.' "

—Shradha Agarwal

CHAPTER 5

Bringing It All Together

"It does not matter how slowly you go as long as you do not stop."

—Confucius

Over the course of these chapters, we have profiled the roles and benefits of grit and the growth mindset, challenged misconceptions about "making an effort," championed the surprising value of making mistakes, and explored the rich and dynamic environments that characterize "gritty" classrooms. At the root of all this is the idea that, to paraphrase George Bernard Shaw, progress is possible with change, but only those who can change their minds can change anything. When learners start with a growth mindset, they can develop the grit traits that will empower them to make sustainable progress toward their life goals.

So how can educators and students synthesize all of these understandings into a practical, straightforward approach that can be applied easily, regularly, and effectively? It would require an approach that was specifically suited to students, compatible with existing curricula and schedules, and would be both kid-friendly yet also worth holding onto as a life strategy for adulthood. Ideally, this approach would make it likelier that learners would sustainably integrate the concepts, practices, and benefits of growth mindsets and grit traits into their daily experiences, both in and beyond the classroom.

That is why, in this closing chapter, we would like to discuss goal-setting and implementation. Specifically, we offer a goal-attainment technique adapted for use in the gritty classroom. (See Part II, Resource 35, I Go for My Goals.)

Along with its growth-mindset orientation and its enlistment of grit traits, this kid-friendly technique also reflects our research into the most widely practiced goal-setting methods and tips, from visualizing and S.M.A.R.T. (goals should be specific, measurable, achievable, realistic, and timely) to personal journaling and 4CF (goals should address clarity, challenge, complexity, commitment, and feedback). Among the methods that we surveyed, none proved more influential and inspiring than that of Mental Contrasting.

As presented by New York University Professors of Psychology Gabriele Oettingen and Peter M. Gollwitzer, Mental Contrasting with Implementation Intentions (MCII) is a technique that addresses both goal-setting and goal achievement. What makes MCII stand out from other such techniques is that it increases the likelihood that people will actually fulfill those goals. Let's take a look at why this is the case and how we came to discover a potential for "partnering" the concepts associated with MCII with those of a growth mindset.

A Better Way to Meet "Gritty" Goals

In mental contrasting to set goals, you imagine having attained "the desired future" and then look at the specific ways in which that future contrasts with your current reality. There have been several studies that have compared mental contrasting with other forms of goal setting, including dwelling (focusing on negative realities) and indulging (focusing on a positive future).

In one study, three groups of students set a goal of attaining specific improvements in their performance of algebra skills. One group focused on current obstacles (dwelling); another group focused on future prospects (indulging); and a third group considered both (mental contrasting). Each group had to elaborate in writing, either about the positive prospects they associated with excelling, the obstacles they experienced in attaining excellence, or in the case of the third group, both the problems and the possibilities. In all three groups, the students were very specific about the problems to be resolved, the benefits that could result, or both.

Two weeks later, teachers for all of the students reported on how much effort each individual student had made in implementing his or her goal and also assessed the student's performance during that period. The students also reported on how engaged, energized, and invested they felt at that stage in terms of attaining their ongoing goal.

Only in the third group—the students who used mental contrasting—did the degree to which they felt engaged or energized, the level of effort they invested, and the results they earned match up with their personal expectations. The other groups reported feeling moderately engaged, making moderate efforts, and achieving moderate results, regardless of their expectations.

Now lest we gloss over an important point, let's go back to the mental contrasting group and take a closer look. The researchers point out that, in this group, the students' reported levels of engagement, efforts, and results in goal attainment *matched their own expectations—high or low*. This suggests to us that a combination of applying mental contrasting *and raising one's expectations* is the key to attaining one's goals. In other words, it all comes back to growth mindset.

Mental Contrasting and Growth Mindset

When we think about students expending effort in the attainment of their goals, it's easy to see how the development of their grit traits will benefit them. Hard work, persistence, conscientiousness, and so on are clear examples of how grit can provide the traction that enables a learner to make progress. But let's also look at the connection between mental contrasting and the growth mindset.

Brain imaging studies have shown that mental contrasting increases activity in those parts of the brain that are associated with working memory, intention formation, episodic memory, and vivid mental imagery formation. To researchers like Anja Achtziger, Oettingen, and several others, this suggests that mental contrasting helps us

- focus on critical information;
- recruit memories of relevant past obstacles and successes, including factors that contributed to each;
- develop greater clarity in assessing current obstacles and delineating the desired future; and
- formulate stronger goal commitment.

Likewise, according to Stanford University researchers at PERTS (Project for Education Research That Scales), the brains of students with a growth mindset have been shown to be significantly more active than those of students with a fixed mindset.

For example, in a study that involved students taking a difficult test, being told they had not done well, and then being offered feedback, the brains of students with a growth mindset were measurably more active than those of students with a fixed mindset.

- Students with a fixed mindset "tuned out" after hearing whether their answers were right or wrong, paying little or no attention to feedback. They also chose to look at the tests of those who had performed worse than them, suggesting a focus on performance rather than process, and on validation over motivation.
- Students with a growth mindset listened attentively to feedback and chose to look at the tests of those who had performed better than they had. They focused on learning as a process that included the ability to improve.

It will come as no surprise that in a follow-up pop quiz, the students with a growth mindset, or process-oriented approach to learning, did better than the students with a fixed mindset, or performance-oriented approach to learning.

What this suggests to us is that the optimal way to attain learning goals is for students to

- begin from, or first transition into, a growth mindset;
- raise their personal expectations, with guidance from their teachers and parents; and
- apply the double-action goal strategy of mental contrasting.

WOOP Up Your Learning

So how does all of this come together amid the day-to-day demands placed on teachers and students? How can you and your students pull together the concepts in this guide and derive the highest benefit from the resources provided here? In order to illustrate how our synthesis of goal-implementation research contributed to some of the resources featured in this book, let's look at how MCII became modified and popularized for the general reader.

Based on the principles of mental contrasting and the planning strategy known formally as *implementation intention* (Gollwitzer), Oettingen developed a general-purpose technique known as WOOP, which she introduced in the best-selling book, *Rethinking Positive Thinking: Inside the New Science of Motivation* (Current, 2014). Easy to understand, remember, and apply, WOOP derives its name from Wish, Outcome, Obstacles, and Plan. Designed to help people transition from "dreaming to doing," WOOP has garnered high praise from reviewers, most notably Dweck and Duckworth.

Inspired by our own experiences with WOOP, and mindful of the needs of gritty learners, we have endeavored to integrate its guiding principles into the kid-friendly tool that we cited previously as Resource 35, I Go for My Goals. We have also incorporated the best practices and aspects of goal implementation into as many of the Grit-to-Go Resources as possible. Thus, the scope of the resources is broad in intention:

- Guiding students toward the optimal starting point, that of a growth mindset
- Setting and meeting students' most important personal learning goals
- Recalling strategies that have helped students overcome obstacles in the past
- Cultivating a growth mindset to envision best possible outcomes
- Acquiring and strengthening the grit traits that will help students sustain their motivation and efforts every step of the way

Growth Mindset and Grit: They're Not Just for Kids

Before you move on to setting goals and drawing on the resources for achieving them, we'd like to leave you with just a few words about the role of responsibility. Throughout this book, we have been discussing the importance of promoting a growth mindset and fostering grit traits among children. At the same time, it behooves all of us—educators, parents, policy makers, elected officials, and other community members—to remember that whatever we seek to foster in children, we must also exemplify as adults.

"I realized that you can change a classroom; you can change a community; and if you can change enough communities, you can change the world."

—Erin Gruwell

Fostering grit is not about foisting an onerous burden onto children and leaving them to sink or swim, nor is it intended as a substitute for meeting children's fundamental daily needs with equity. It does not make it acceptable to underfund a school or to ignore socioeconomic challenges within a community.

Modeling grit and cultivating the growth mindset are very much about empowering children to develop the full range of their human potential. Thus, each of us must engage our own grit traits as we work for the betterment of ourselves and the betterment of others. We do this collectively by many means:

- Listening for the good in others' ideas (*open-mindedness*)
- Acknowledging what others contribute to our lives (*gratitude*)
- Letting go of cynicism and living from the heart (*optimism*)
- Committing to long-term progress for all instead of quick fixes for a few (*delayed gratification*)
- Striving to deliver the most widely beneficial outcomes of our labor (*hard work*)
- Being attentive to the details of our day's biggest priorities (*conscientiousness*)
- Stepping out of our comfort zones, from sharing our talents to standing up to injustice (*courage*)
- Speaking and acting responsively, not reactively (*self-control*)
- Practicing, day by day, steps that define being on our right path (*persistence*)
- Pursuing our worthiest goals while rising to life's challenges (*perseverance*)
- Recovering from disappointment, setbacks, and loss (*resilience*)
- Holding fast to our ideals and principles (*tenacity*)
- Acting with consideration of our neighbors, locally and globally (*social intelligence*)

TAKE-AWAYS: Setting and Achieving Goals

- The most effective goal-setting and attainment tool is one that begins with growth mindset and then leverages the power of grit traits.
- In mental contrasting, a student contrasts his or her ideal outcome with the current realities.
- Raised expectations have been shown to play a key role in attaining the desired goal.
- Strengthening grit traits will help students sustain their motivation and efforts.
- What we foster in students, we must cultivate in ourselves.

PART II

Grit-to-Go Reproducible Resources

I
Meet the Mindsets

"Mary, Mary, it's extraordinary, how does your mindset grow?" From rhymes to reason, myths to misconceptions, our personal lore of beliefs about the mind affects our ability to learn.

To open our resource section, you'll find two reproducible letters that you can send home. The first is a brief explanation of mindsets that students can personalize. The second letter is from you. It provides an overview of grit along with ideas for grit-building at home.

Date: ____________________

Dear ________________________________,

We are learning about the brain and how it grows. Long ago, scientists thought people could not become any more intelligent than they already were. They believed that you were either born smart, or you were not.

Today, we know that the brain is like a muscle. The more you use it, the smarter you get. My brain can actually *grow* the more I learn. Even when I make a mistake, my brain can use that information to help me learn.

We are also learning about mindsets. A **mindset** is a belief that people have about their intelligence.

- Someone with a **fixed mindset** believes there is only so much he can learn. He may say things like, “I can’t,” “It’s too hard,” and “I’m just not good at that subject.”
- Someone with a **growth mindset** believes she can always learn more. She says things like, “I can,” “I’ll keep trying,” and “I can get better at that subject if I practice.”
- Most people have a mix of mindsets. They may believe that they can grow in some ways, but they feel stuck in other ways.

I feel ____ to learn

____.

I believe that ____.

Sincerely,

____

Date:

Dear Families,

I'm pleased to welcome you and your child to my "gritty" classroom. Research by Angela Duckworth, Ph.D., Carol Dweck, Ph.D., and other scientists and educators has revealed some very encouraging findings about grit.

Grit, or *perseverance and passion for short- and long-term goals* is a better predictor of success than IQ. People with grit also make a habit of meeting short-term goals. When we develop grit—the traits we need to meet challenges, to recover from setbacks, and to stay focused on goals—we greatly increase our ability to succeed in life.

You probably know several people in your life who are "gritty," from grandparents to very young children. Resilient and optimistic, they persist in giving their best effort, even when they meet with obstacles.

Within the framework of our current curriculum, your children will have the opportunity to develop their grit skills in the classroom. They will also discover strategies for learning and enjoying subjects they may now find difficult. Here are some ways to help your child in this process:

- **Praise their efforts.** Instead of emphasizing how smart or gifted they are, say, "You worked hard!" or ask them to talk about the specific efforts they made. Focusing on the process of learning makes children more willing to learn new things since it removes the pressure on them to be perfect.
- **Let your child see that making mistakes is part of learning.** No one becomes an expert on the first attempt. No team wins every game. Invite your child to talk about mistakes and failures. Praise them for trying again. Allow them to learn from consequences.
- **Encourage positive self-talk.** If your child says, "I'm just no good at (*fill in the blank*)," change the focus to, "I can't do it yet, but I can practice and get better." Share ideas about how they can improve.
- **Invite thinking "out loud."** Ask your child to explain how they went about completing an assignment or a problem.
- **Remind your child that the brain can grow.** Every time the brain learns something new, even when it makes and corrects a mistake, it forms new pathways.
- **Talk about your own goals and efforts.** Show your child that learning is a lifelong process.

Sincerely,

MINDSETS

The beliefs that people form about their intelligence.

Fixed Mindset

People have a fixed amount of intelligence or skill.

Growth Mindset

People can always learn more.

Informal Growth Mindset Self-Assessment

Directions: Assign a number, 1–5, to indicate your degree of agreement or disagreement with each "I" mindset statement.

1 2 3 4 5

- **1** Not true of me
- **2** Rarely true of me
- **3** Sometimes true of me
- **4** Defines me
- **5** Strongly defines me

1. I am optimistic.	
2. I am always up to a challenge.	
3. I identify my own strengths and weaknesses.	
4. I believe I always have something to learn.	
5. I think of myself as always evolving.	
6. I stretch myself when learning something new.	
7. I have the persistence to learn something over a longer time period.	
8. I try doing things I couldn't do before.	
9. I view mistakes as learning opportunities.	
10. I am always prepared and punctual.	
Add the numbers and divide the sum by 10 to determine your score. Circle your score on the scale.	

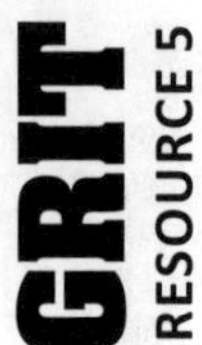

WHAT'S IN YOUR MINDSET?

Write beliefs that go with each mindset.

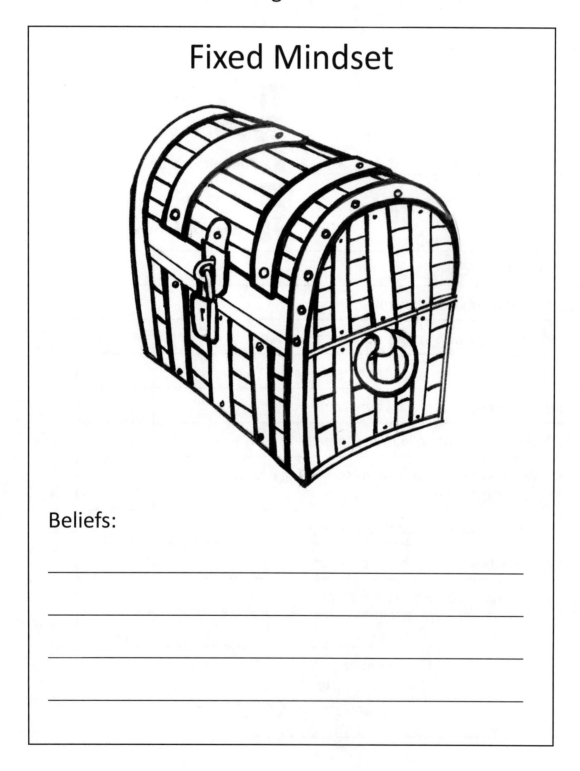

Fixed Mindset

Beliefs:

____

____

____

____

Growth Mindset

Beliefs:

2
Introducing Grit

Grit is a better predictor than IQ of long-term achievement.
What is grit and who can benefit from it?

Introduce Grit Traits

Give students the resources to understand the traits that foster grit and a growth mindset. The order in which you introduce the grit traits is up to you. After all, they are interconnected. Here are some options designed for easy integration into your regular curriculum.

- Display the Grit Traits Poster (Resource 8). Let students know that you will be exploring each of the traits throughout the year.
- Introduce one new grit trait per week. This will allow students to cycle through the grit traits at least twice during the academic year.
- Introduce grit traits gradually by relating them to applicable themed units and reading selections from your existing lesson plans. See The Good Grit Reading List, page 152, for suggestions.
- Display a Grit Trait of the Week where all students can see it (Resource 31). Take advantage of teachable moments about that trait during the week.

Tap into Kids' Knowledge. As a general rule, it's more productive to activate students' prior knowledge about a trait before supplying them with a definition, particularly when the trait vocabulary is unfamiliar. While terms like *delayed gratification* and *conscientiousness* are not exactly household words for younger students, they already know more about such traits than they may initially realize.

Explore the Resources. To help keep the introductions fun and effective, Resources 18–49 offer scenarios, comparisons, and questions designed to spark children's ideas about how the traits impact their lives in and beyond the classroom. Depending on students' readiness and fluency, you can present these resources as guided readings for the whole class or have students explore the resources in pairs, with little or no outside assistance.

Share the Science. Whenever possible, give students opportunities to get some idea of what scientists are discovering about the functions or benefits of grit traits. (Using kid-friendly language, we have also summarized many of these benefits on the resources themselves.) With a bit of judicious searching, you can zero in on concise, accessible, and reputable scientific news reports and multimedia presentations.

For example, it's one thing to discuss delayed gratification, but nothing drives home the concept like letting students see for themselves what is perhaps the most famous experiment conducted on the subject—the Marshmallow Test. You will find several classroom-appropriate videos about it online, including on YouTube:

www.youtube.com/watch?v=QX_oy9614HQ

Encourage students to share what they observe, including how several of the children in the video use strategies to help them delay the gratification of receiving that second marshmallow. Students can also relate what they see to the information on their resources.

Some other examples of the "shareable science" behind the grit traits include:

- A helpful 10-point list of **tenacity** behaviors and strategies, in "Why Academic Tenacity Matters," an article that first appeared in *Scientific American*: blogs.scientificamerican.com/beautiful-minds/why-academic-tenacity-matters
- An engaging talk by Angela Duckworth, Ph.D., in which she presents **self-control** strategies for school-age children: youtube/X1euhGUKIRc
- An easy-to-read science report about **optimism**, "Kids as Young as 5 See Benefits of Positive Thinking," by Remy Melina, which was first published in LiveScience.com: www.livescience.com/17596-young-children-positive-thinking.html
- Brief biographical vignettes about scientists, such as the way Nobel Prize-winning biologist John Gurdon learned a childhood lesson about **perseverance**. (See Resource 26.)
- Examples of grit traits in action, as in "The Perseverance Walk," a 5th-grade classroom assignment that went viral after it was first posted on Edutopia.com: www.youtube.com/watch?v=YRBblCgYyJM

Relate the Trait to Classroom Content. You can use a grit trait, such as delayed gratification, or patience, to add context about a fictional character or actual person that your students are studying. Examples:

- (Fiction) The first two pigs built their homes the easy way, and their homes didn't last. But the third little pig took the time to build his house out of brick. He probably wanted a house right away, but he delayed gratification in order to have a better, stronger house.
- (Nonfiction) In 1922, Bessie Coleman became the world's first black woman to earn a pilot's license. When American flying schools refused to accept her, she decided to study in France. To do this, she first had to learn the French language and work as a manicurist to save up the money to travel. She delayed doing the thing she liked to do—fly a plane—in order to gain the greater reward of becoming an officially licensed pilot.

Informal Grit Trait Self-Assessment

Directions: Assign a number, 1–5, to indicate your degree of agreement or disagreement with each "I" grit trait statement.

1 2 3 4 5

- **1** Not true of me
- **2** Rarely true of me
- **3** Sometimes true of me
- **4** Defines me
- **5** Strongly defines me

1. I exhibit a great deal of self-control.	
2. I persist even when things are difficult.	
3. I am tenacious and stay-the-course.	
4. I am resilient and recover from setbacks and disappointments.	
5. I have a strong work ethic.	
6. I practice delayed gratification.	
7. I persevere and don't easily quit.	
8. I am an optimistic person.	
9. I am open-minded to new ideas and change.	
10. I am always conscientious about my work.	
11. I consider myself socially intelligent.	
12. I am grateful and practice gratitude every day.	
13. I consider myself a courageous person.	
Add the numbers and divide the sum by 13 to determine your score. Circle your score on the scale.	

GRIT TRAITS

Self-control (willpower)

Persistence

Tenacity

RESILIENCE

Hard work

Courage

Continued on next page

Delayed gratification

Perseverance

Open-mindedness

Optimism

Conscientiousness

Gratitude

Social intelligence

Grit-Trait Cards for "Gritty" Kids

Students can use these cards in a variety of ways, including as daily reminders or journal entries; building class anthologies; trading them with other students; incorporating them into artwork and essays; and posting on school displays.

Self-control (willpower) I control my feelings and my actions.

Date: ______________________

My example: ____

____

____

Persistence I can continue to work at something, even when it gets difficult.

Date: ______________________

My example: ____

____

____

Tenacity When something is important, I hold onto it. I can be tenacious about information I've learned, a promise that I have made, or a goal that I have set.

Date: ______________________

My example: ____

____

____

Continued on next page

Resilience When things change or something unpleasant happens, I learn how to adjust and return to a positive state of mind.

Date: ______________________

My example: ____

____

____

Hard work Every day, I make a steady effort for the good.

Date: ______________________

My example: ____

____

____

Delayed gratification I can wait! Instead of settling for a small reward right now, I first do what's important. Then I can enjoy a bigger and better reward later.

Date: ______________________

My example: ____

____

____

Gratitude I say thank you. I take time to appreciate everything I have in my life.

Date: ______________________

My example: ____

____

____

Perseverance I keep trying, even when I make mistakes or feel discouraged.

Date: ______________________________

My example: ____

____

____

Open-mindedness I'm eager to learn about new ideas. I'm willing to try new ways of doing things.

Date: ______________________________

My example: ____

____

____

Optimism I have hopes for the future. I'm cheerful. I look for the good in things and people.

Date: ______________________________

My example: ____

____

____

Conscientiousness I pay careful attention to details and directions.

Date: ______________________________

My example: ____

____

____

Continued on next page

Social intelligence I cooperate with my teacher and my classmates. I help people in my family and my community.

Date: ______________________________

My example: ______________________________

____

____

Courage I am willing to face difficulties. I am not afraid of making mistakes because I know that I can learn from them.

Date: ______________________________

My example: ______________________________

____

____

Grit Through the Ages:
Traditional Character Traits

Traditional character traits usually center around ethical and community values. Discussions of themed fiction and nonfiction selections of most Reading and Social Studies programs offer excellent starting points for exploring such traits, which may include, but are not limited to:

- Honesty
- Integrity
- Responsibility
- Compassion
- Empathy
- Caring
- Fairness
- Respect
- Kindness
- Charity
- Good citizenship
- Patriotism

Character Traits for Global Citizens. As today's graduates enter a globally connected world of markets, ideas, and endeavors, many students will also benefit from exploring such emerging character qualities as social consciousness, cultural sensitivity, and environmental awareness. To foster critical thinking, encourage your students to discuss the significance of such qualities and how they arise from, relate to, or compete with more time-honored character traits.

"People grow through experience if they meet life honestly and courageously. This is how character is built."

—Eleanor Roosevelt

3
My Growing Brain

A growing body of knowledge about the brain makes clear that its development is a lifelong process. That's good news for everybody.

Hi, I'm Your Brain!

Help students understand that their brains are growing:

- Read aloud a book like *Your Fantastic Elastic Brain*, by JoAnn Deak, Ph.D., and Sarah Ackerley (Little Pickle Press, 2010). Get students talking about the key concepts, especially the fact that the brain grows and changes.

- Ask students what they know about the brain. Or, engage students in brainstorming several things they know how to do as living beings, such as walk, talk, think, breathe, run, smell, taste, and so on. Ask: *How do you know how to do these things? Which ones can you do without even trying? Which ones do you need to decide to do?* Invite students to list their ideas.

- Introduce the idea of a growth mindset. Ask: *Now that you know that your brain grows and changes the more you use it, how does that make you feel about learning?*

- Students can use the student version of the resource to show what they have learned.

- Students will enjoy *The Adventures of Ned the Neuron*, available as both an app and an e-book on iTunes or direct from the publisher, Kizoom. While it gets a little carried away by the fun of turning a neuron into a character, it does also illustrate the idea of neurons as carrying messages to and from the brain and has drawn praise from the *Berkeley Science Review*, the Society for Neuroscience, and other science organizations.

  www.kizoomlabs.com/products/the-adventures-of-ned-the-neuron

Hi, I'm Your Brain!

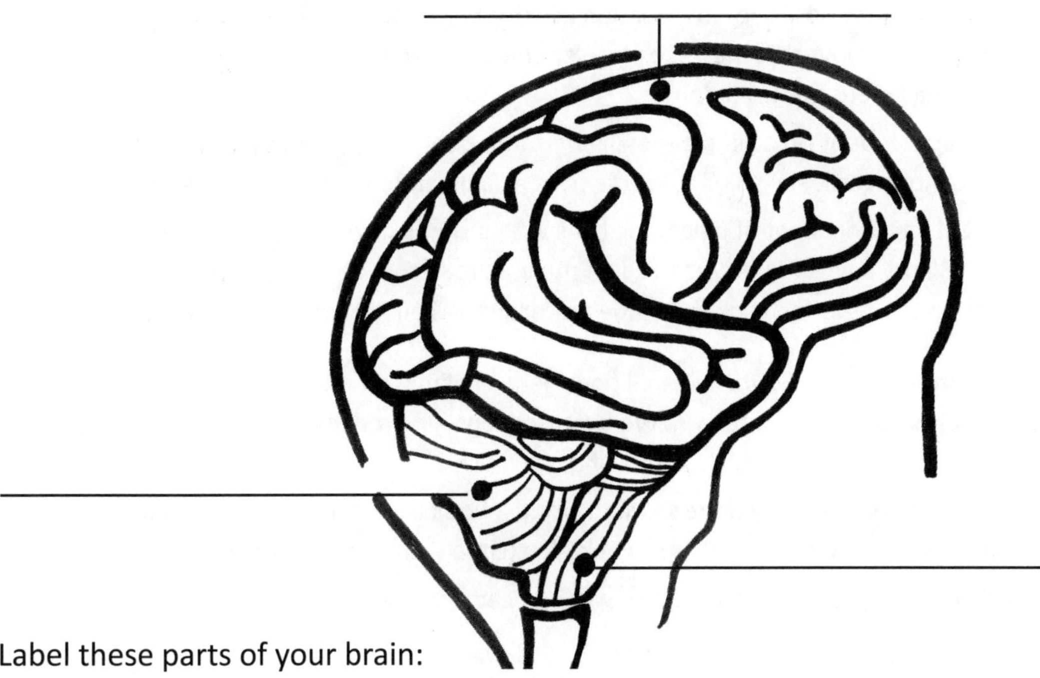

Label these parts of your brain:

Cerebellum **Cerebrum** **Medulla or Brain Stem**	breathe, digest sense, think, imagine balance, move, learn

Describe how you use these parts of your brain.

Cerebellum ____

____

Cerebrum ____

____

Medulla ____

____

Know Your Neurons

Introduce the Function of Neurons.

- Ask students: How does information get from place to place? Invite them to brainstorm ways that messages are sent and received. Examples: phone calls, emails, passing a note, conversation.
- Engage students in a simple messaging game or activity, such as playing the telephone game, in which students sit in a circle and repeat a whispered prompt.
- Label an assortment of ping pong balls with a simple prompt such as "Move," "Smile," or "Blink." Invite volunteers to catch the ball, read the message, and act out the prompt. It is perfectly okay if students "drop the ball" and need to pick it up.

Display an Image of a Neuron. (You'll find them available on the Internet.)
Tell students that neurons carry nerve impulses that function like messages in our bodies. Follow some of these suggestions to elaborate on this.

- If you haven't already done so, read aloud a book like *Your Fantastic Elastic Brain*, by JoAnn Deak, Ph.D., and Sarah Ackerley (Little Pickle Press, 2010).
- Talk about what happened in the game of catch you just played:
  - Your eye sees the ball that I throw.
  - Your eye sends a message to the visual cortex of your brain.
  - The visual cortex sends a message to a neuron in your spinal cord.
  - The neuron in your spinal cord sends a message to the muscle cells in your hand.
  - The muscles in your hand catch the ball.
- Invite students to role play or illustrate these steps.

Explain What Neurons Do. Your neurons helped send all these messages. A neuron is a cell that carries messages between your brain and other parts of your body.

Share Some Fun Facts with Students.

- Invite kids to guess how many miles per hour a neuron can send nerve signals to and from the brain? (Answer: Up to 200 miles per hour)
- Invite kids to guess how many neurons they have in their brain. (Answer: The human brain contains about 100 billion neurons.)
- Point out the fibers (dendrites) that grow out of a neuron and resemble the branches of a tree. Explain: Dendrites grow out of your neurons whenever you learn something, including when you listen, write, speak, or practice.

Know Your Neurons

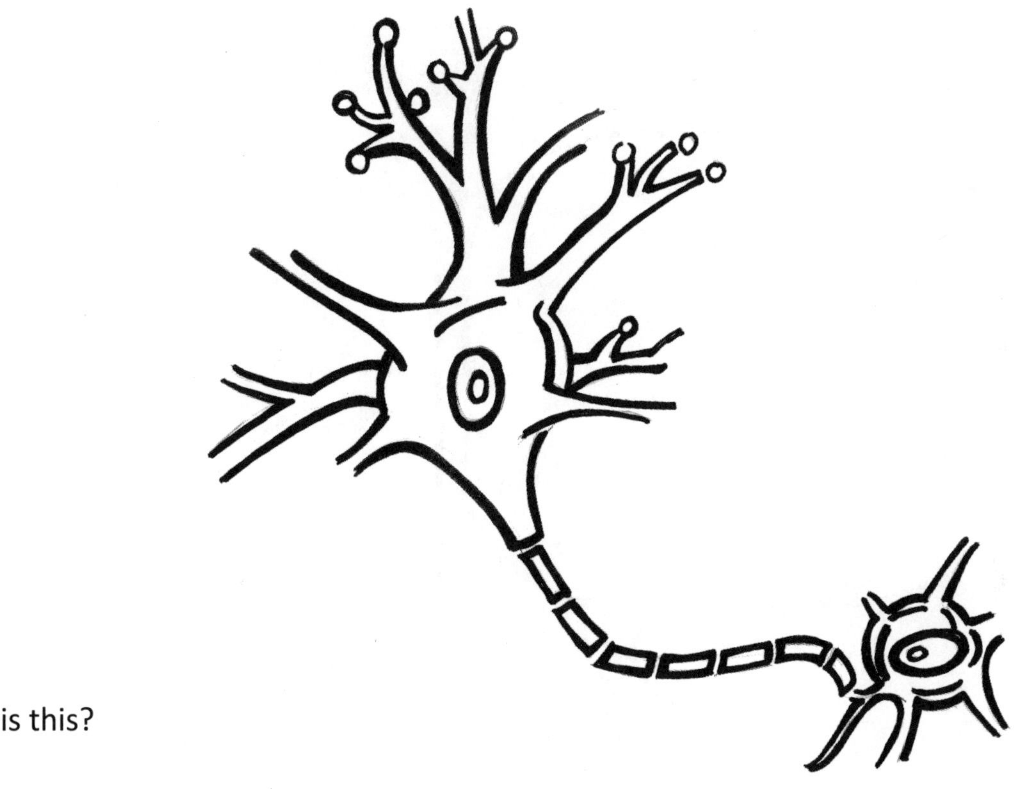

What is this?

What does it do?

Add to your picture. Show what grows out of a neuron whenever you learn something. (Hint: It looks like the branches of a tree.)

Ways that I grow my brain:

I listen to ____.

I write about ______________________________________.

I talk about _______________________________________.

I practice ____.

Are You Stuck?

Someone who has a **fixed mindset** says:

Someone who has a **growth mindset** says:

Trade drawings with a partner.

Take turns reading aloud the speech balloons.

Share what you would say in reply.

What Did You Do for Your Brain This Week?

Healthy Habits

I know that a healthy brain is part of a healthy body.
So I practiced these healthy habits or activities:

1. ______________________________

2. ______________________________

3. ______________________________

Brain-Friendly Messages

I also "fed" my brain good messages:

1. ______________________________

2. ______________________________

3. ______________________________

Brain-Building Ideas

I know that new information helps my brain grow.

1. I grew my brain by learning about ______________________________.

2. I learned that ______________________________.

3. I want to learn about ______________________________.

What if I Make a Mistake?

Distribute the student pages of Resources 15 and 16. Allow students a few minutes to read the Discover paragraphs on Resource 15 and respond to the questions.

Introduce the Activity. Ask students to briefly share how they feel whenever they make a mistake in math. Remind them that making mistakes is part of how we learn.

Ask. *Did you know that every time we make a mistake in math it has a physical effect on our brain?* You can invite students to create a list of possible effects based on their guesses.

Share the Science. Show students a brief video that shows synapses firing as information is passed from neuron to neuron in the brain. For example:
www.istockphoto.com/video/firing-neurons-30235832?st=34b52d9

At this point you can have students watch the 3-minute video in which Jo Boaler explains the positive effect of making a mistake in math:
www.youtube.com/watch?v=btDHUHZ6fAw

Alternatively, you can tell students that scientists have discovered that every time we make a mistake in math, the brain grows a new synapse.

Point out the Image. Point out the image of a neuron on Resource 16 and then ask students:
Guess what happens when we think about the mistake again?
Give students a moment to respond. *Yes, we grow a new synapse!*

So what do you now know about making mistakes in math?
Encourage students to share their conclusions as they complete their drawings.

Everyone Makes Mistakes

Consider. How do you feel when you make a mistake in math or another subject? What do you say to yourself?

____

____

Discover. Read the following short passage, "Even a Genius Makes Mistakes."

Everybody makes mistakes. Even one of the smartest scientists in the world, Albert Einstein, made mistakes. Some of Einstein's mistakes were in math. He made mistakes even after he became a scientist.

However, making mistakes did not stop Einstein. They helped him learn. He would think about his mistakes and try again. After many years, Einstein figured out new ideas about the way that space, time, light, and movement work. As Einstein later said, "Anyone who has never made a mistake has never tried anything new."

Some scientists today believe that Einstein did not see every single one of his mistakes. No one is perfect, not even Einstein! Because he persevered, however, people today continue to learn from him.

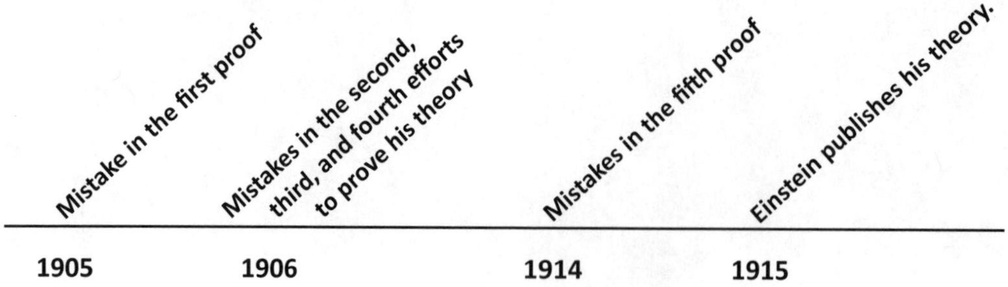

Respond. Now that you have read this passage, how do you feel about making mistakes as you learn? What can you tell yourself when you make a mistake?

____

____

____

____

____

____

____

____

____

____

____

____

More to Explore. For an easy and engaging introduction to Albert Einstein's work, read *On a Beam of Light: A Story of Albert Einstein*, by Jennifer Berne (Author) and Vladimir Radunsky (Illustrator); Chronicle Books, 2013.

Timeline adapted from *Einstein's Mistakes: The Human Failings of Genius*, by Hans C. Ohanian; W.W. Norton & Company, 2008.)

What If I Make a Mistake?

Review. Every time you learn new information, it causes your brain to grow. Look at the neuron below. The lines that look like branches are called dendrites. Every time you learn something, your neurons grow more dendrites.

Consider. What do you think happens to your brain when you make a mistake? For example, what if you make a mistake in math? Would you like to guess? Don't worry about whether your guess is right or wrong.

____

____

____

Respond. What have you learned? Were you surprised?

____

____

____

Focus: Your Ticket to the "Train" of Thought

Attention! Scientists report that the average human attention span keeps getting shorter. How do they know? Researchers for Microsoft surveyed 2,000 people in North America and studied the brain activity of 112 others. They looked at how long people could pay attention to something before they responded to outside distractions.

They discovered that between the years 2000 and 2013, the average human attention span fell from 12 seconds to just 8 seconds. That's one second shorter than the average attention span of a *goldfish!*

It seems that too many people get distracted by mobile devices, TV, background noise, and other interruptions. Their train of thought keeps getting bumped off track. Each time they are interrupted, it takes more and more time and brain power to get back on board. As a result, people who are constantly distracted tend to feel tired, wonder where the day went, and have trouble completing tasks.

Tip:

The next time you feel distracted, try this. Take a deep breath and slowly breathe out. This helps send more oxygen to your brain and will refresh your attention.

Continued on next page

Now for the Good News. Just as you can grow your brain by actively learning and thinking, you can also grow your focus. Here's how:

First, answer a few questions:

- When and where do you feel distracted?
- What are some things that distract you?
- When you are doing homework, what "derails" your train of thought?
- What feelings do you experience because of these distractions?

Next, turn and talk about your answers with a partner. Then brainstorm solutions by answering these questions together:

- What are some ways to show that you are listening carefully in class?
- How else can you keep track of important ideas and information?
- When you are doing homework,
  * What should you put away or turn off?
  * What items do you need in order to do the assignment?
  * Where and how should you sit in order to stay focused?

4

Grit Really Gets Me Going!

Along with modeling, one of the best ways to teach grit traits to students is sharing the terms and examples, science connections, and real-world applications.

Open-mindedness: Welcome New Ideas

Imagine a group of students brainstorming topics to read about. Several students have shared ideas. Read their ideas and then read how two students reacted to those ideas.

Topic Ideas	What Sam Said	What Chris Said
Can Animals Communicate?	"That's an interesting question! Should we narrow it down to one or two animals?"	"Who cares? I'm not interested."
Kinds of Bears	"I'm not sure. Can you tell me more about that idea?"	"No, that sounds boring."
How Computers Work	"That might be challenging, but I'd be willing to try."	"No way, that's too hard."
Exploring Mars	"Great idea! Thanks for explaining it in more detail."	"I wasn't listening."

What do you notice about how Sam reacted? What do you notice about how Chris reacted? Who was more willing to consider other people's ideas? How can you tell?

____

____

____

____

____

____

____

____

What Is Open-mindedness? In the scene you just read, one student shut down every idea. Sometimes he said no right away. Sometimes he didn't even listen. He was close-minded.

The other student was open-minded. Open-mindedness means that you are willing to listen and learn. It doesn't mean that you have to agree with every idea. But before you make up your mind, you learn more about the idea, and you think carefully about it.

More About Open-mindedness. Scientific discoveries, inventions, and the human search for knowledge all depend on open-mindedness. If nobody considered new ideas, we would never make any progress. Open-mindedness also helps people with different ideas get along in the world.

Practice Open-mindedness. Make a list of music, games, or books that you **dislike**. Then find someone in your class who **likes** something on your list. Ask that person to tell you what he or she likes about it. Just listen carefully. Even if you still disagree, what are one or two good ideas that he or she shared?

______________________ ______________________

______________________ ______________________

______________________ ______________________

______________________ ______________________

______________________ ______________________

Courage: Take Action

Sometimes we know what to do, but we just can't seem to do it. Read this scene.

Jan and Kim are new students at Oak School. All week, Jan never raises her hand, even though she knows many of the answers. She is afraid of making mistakes.

Kim feels nervous, too. She raises her hand anyway. Sometimes her answers are right; sometimes they are wrong. By finding the courage to raise her hand, Kim begins to feel more at ease in the new school. She notices that everybody in the class makes mistakes now and then.

One day Jan notices that when students make a mistake, nothing terrible happens. The teacher just asks them more questions to help them think through their ideas and get to the best answer. Sometimes there is even more than one right answer! That day, Jan takes a deep breath and raises her hand.

Turn and Talk. With a partner, take turns sharing about a time when you

- had to speak or write in front of the class,
- wanted to join in a game at recess, or
- saw someone causing harm at school.

How did you feel? What were you afraid of or nervous about? What did you do? What happened as a result? How was your experience like or unlike Kim's or Jan's?

What Is Courage? Sometimes people think that courage means you don't feel any fear. In fact, courage means that you are willing to take the right action and to feel any fear that goes with it.

Courage is a trait that each of us can develop. One of the best ways to find your courage is to help someone else find *his* courage. If you know someone who feels shy or afraid about doing the right thing, you can en<u>courage</u> him.

Explore the Science. Scientists have discovered that a part of your brain becomes more active when you act with courage, even if you still feel afraid. They believe that this brain activity helps you gain more control over your behavior. In other words, each time you show courage, it gets easier.

Practice Courage. Complete the following Courage statement. Read aloud and display your statement in the classroom.

In my opinion, students at school may sometimes feel afraid to ____________

____.

I promise that when they do, I will _______________________________________.

Even if they make a mistake, I won't ______________________________________.

I want to encourage others to ____.

I want to have the courage to ____.

Optimism: Train Your Brain Power!

Two students are waiting for the school bus when it starts to rain. Pete frowns and says, "Oh no! Now I have to carry this stupid umbrella." Omar smiles and says, "Oh wow! I'm so glad I have an umbrella."

- How does Pete feel about the rain? What does Pete focus on?
- How does Omar feel about the rain? What does Omar focus on?

What Is Optimism? In the scene you just read, two students look at the same event, but they see it in two different ways. Some people mostly notice the *good* in life. They have **optimism**. Some people mostly notice the *bad* in life. They have **pessimism**.

Turn and Talk. With a partner, share your ideas about how someone with pessimism might react to the following events. Then show how someone with optimism might react.

Event	Pessimism	Optimism
Getting an apple with a tiny worm in it	"It's ruined!"	"I can slice off that part of the apple."
Not doing well on a test		
Missing the school bus		

Take a "Good Look." Even someone who is pessimistic can become optimistic. That's because optimism is a way of thinking. It is a skill that anyone can learn. The way you look at everyday events is important.

Explore the Science. Optimism "wakes up" a part of your brain called the amygdala (uh-MIG-duh-luh). Being optimistic trains that part of your brain to pay more attention to good things, and less attention to bad things. This, in turn, lowers stress and boosts physical health. When you face problems with optimism, you can find solutions, instead of feeling helpless.

Practice Optimism. Write down three things that have gone well today. With a partner, take turns reading the items on your list. Listen carefully to each other. How are your lists alike? How are they different? How does it make you feel to focus on the things that went well?

1. ____

____

____

2. ____

____

____

3. ____

____

____

Delayed Gratification:
Keep Your Eyes on the Prize

Throughout life, there are things we want to do or have. Think of things people look forward to and make a list. It might include items such as:

- A birthday, holiday, or family vacation
- Getting a new toy or other special treat
- Going to college
- Being able to drive a car
- Being able to do something really well

Circle three things on your list that you look forward to doing or having.

What Is Delayed Gratification? This is when you don't just think about what you want right now, you also think about what you want in the future. You could also call this wise waiting.

Short-Term Wants: I WANT THIS NOW	Long-Term Wants: I WANT THIS SOME DAY
A candy bar that costs $2	A bike that costs $120
To play instead of doing homework	To go to college and get a job as a video game designer

Wise Waiting. Wise waiting is also active waiting because once you know which things on your "WANT" list are the most important, you can turn them into goals. You can then take steps toward your goals every day.

Turn and Talk. With a partner, talk about the examples in the chart. For example: Let's say you really want the bike. What happens if every time you have $2, you (A) spend it on candy or (B) save it toward the cost of the bike?

Add to the Chart. What is something you want right now? What is something you want some day? Which is more important to you? Why? Are you willing to practice wise waiting? What steps are you willing to take while you wait?

Explore the Science. Find an online video about the famous Marshmallow Test. In it, children were given a choice between one marshmallow right away, or two marshmallows later—if they could wait until the tester returned. For 15 minutes, each child sat alone in a room staring right at a delicious marshmallow. How do you think you would do?

Why the Science Matters. When researchers did follow-up studies over many years, they discovered something interesting. The children who were able to wait 15 minutes for the second marshmallow did better in school and had more success in life. Instead of settling for small rewards right away (instant gratification), they focused on achieving the bigger rewards that take more time.

Tip: *Scientists also learned a great tip from kids. The kids who were good at waiting passed the time by focusing on other things! So the next time you are feeling impatient or bored, find a good book to read or spend a few minutes figuring out a math problem. It really works!*

Self-Control: Set Some Rules

Being a human is interesting. Sometimes, we just want to roar like a lion or to act as lively as a monkey. For example, when we are little babies, we may cry as loud as we want whenever and wherever we want. That's because we don't know what else to do.

As we grow, we learn many helpful ways to control the way we act. This doesn't just help people around us feel happier. It helps us feel happier, too.

Turn and Talk. For example, imagine that you felt really, really mad. Maybe you dropped your popcorn on the way into the movie theatre. Imagine that the movie has started. Would you:

- Shout "I want more popcorn" over and over?
- Say nothing at all and just get madder and madder?
- Whisper to your friend, "May I please share some of your popcorn?"

Talk over your choice with a partner. What do you think would happen in each of the three cases above? Why?

What Is Self-Control? When we practice self-control, we don't **stop** our feelings. We **take care** of them. We set rules that let us feel our feelings and still do what we need to do. Using the chart, work with your partner to explore examples like these:

- Recall a time when you were having fun playing outside and your parents told you that it was time to come in. How did you react when you had to stop? Why?
- On the other hand, what would happen if your parents let you stay outside and you played all night? How would you start to feel as it got later and later? How would you feel at school the next day? Why?

Explore Self-Control. Discuss the following examples with your partner.

Self-control scenarios	What can happen if I don't use self-control	Ways that I can use self-control
I use social media during my study time.		
My parents tell me to clean up my room, which has been getting messier every day.		
I feel upset with a classmate.		
I don't feel like paying attention during one of my classes.		

Apply the Science. A scientist named Angela Duckworth discovered that students can improve their self-control in many ways. For example, if you are having trouble paying attention, you can:

- Tidy up your desk first, to put away anything that might distract you.
- Keep your eyes on the teacher or student who is speaking. It will make it easier for you to listen and think about new information.

Tip:

Here's a great strategy to help you practice self-control: Plan something fun for yourself that you will only do if you achieve your self-control goal all week.

Gratitude: Thanking Helps Your Thinking!

One of the first lessons we learn as children is how to say "Thank you." What are some reasons you thank someone?

- I say thank you to __________________ when _____________________.
- I say thank you to __________________ when _____________________.
- I say thank you to __________________ when _____________________.

On Thanksgiving Day, people often share why they are thankful about big and little things in their lives. We can express our thankfulness, or gratitude, every day. What are some big or little things that you are thankful for? List them here.

Tip: *Get into the "Gritty Gratitude" habit! Start a gratitude list. Every day, add something to the list. Your reasons for gratitude can be big or small. "I feel grateful for the school bus when it is rainy." "I feel grateful that I figured out that tricky math question!"*

____

____

____

____

____

____

What Is Gratitude? Gratitude is another word for thankfulness. We have Thanksgiving Day once a year, but we can celebrate gratitude every day!

Explore the Science. Gratitude is good for your brain. Scientists have discovered that even just thinking about gratitude affects our brain in ways that make us feel happier.

Persistence: Just One More Try!

Do you remember the first time you learned to tie your shoes or ride a bike? Did you do everything perfectly the first time? Of course not! But you knew that you'd succeed if you just kept trying.

Think about how babies learn to walk. There are many steps along the way:

- First, they learn how to stand up.
- Then, they learn how to ______________________________.
- Next, they start walking. At first, the way they walk is ______________
  ____.
- After many tries, the way they walk is ______________________.

Learning how to walk is one of our first lessons in persistence.

What Is Persistence? When you are persistent about learning, you try something over and over again until you become better at it. You don't give up after one or two tries. Instead, you figure out what you need to do to improve. You keep practicing.

Apply the Science. Scientists report that most people can think up a higher number of solutions to problems than they realize. All they have to do is persist at the task a little longer. When you are answering a lot of homework questions, you may sometimes feel like stopping before you are done. Persist in doing a few more. Or persist in redoing a question that you got wrong before. You may be surprised at all the ways this can help you.

Continued on next page

Try This with a Partner.

- Can you make up **three words** using letters in the word ELEPHANT?

____

____

____

- Can you make up **five more word**s using letters in the word ELEPHANT?

____

____

____

____

____

- How many more words do you think you could make using the letters in the word ELEPHANT? 3 more? 5 more? 10 more?

____

____

____

In fact, you can make more than 50 common words from the letters in the word ELEPHANT.

Why Is Persistence Important? In school and in life, we often have to "try, try again." Sometimes we think that we only have one or two good tries to make before we decide to give up. But as the ELEPHANT words show, the more we try, the better our results will be.

Resilience: Bounce Back Up!

Think about these two everyday objects:

- A raw egg
- A rubber ball

What happens if you drop the egg? What happens if you drop the ball?

What Is Resilience? When things go wrong, it's normal to feel upset. But even when big things in life go wrong, you are not "broken." You can use your resilience. That's your ability to feel better again.

Resilient people know that even when life seems hard, it will get better again. If they fall down, they get right back up. They bounce back like a rubber ball.

Turn and Talk. With a partner, brainstorm ideas for the chart. First, think about a setback, or disappointment. Then think about what someone who has resilience would say. Remember, resilient people don't stay down for long.

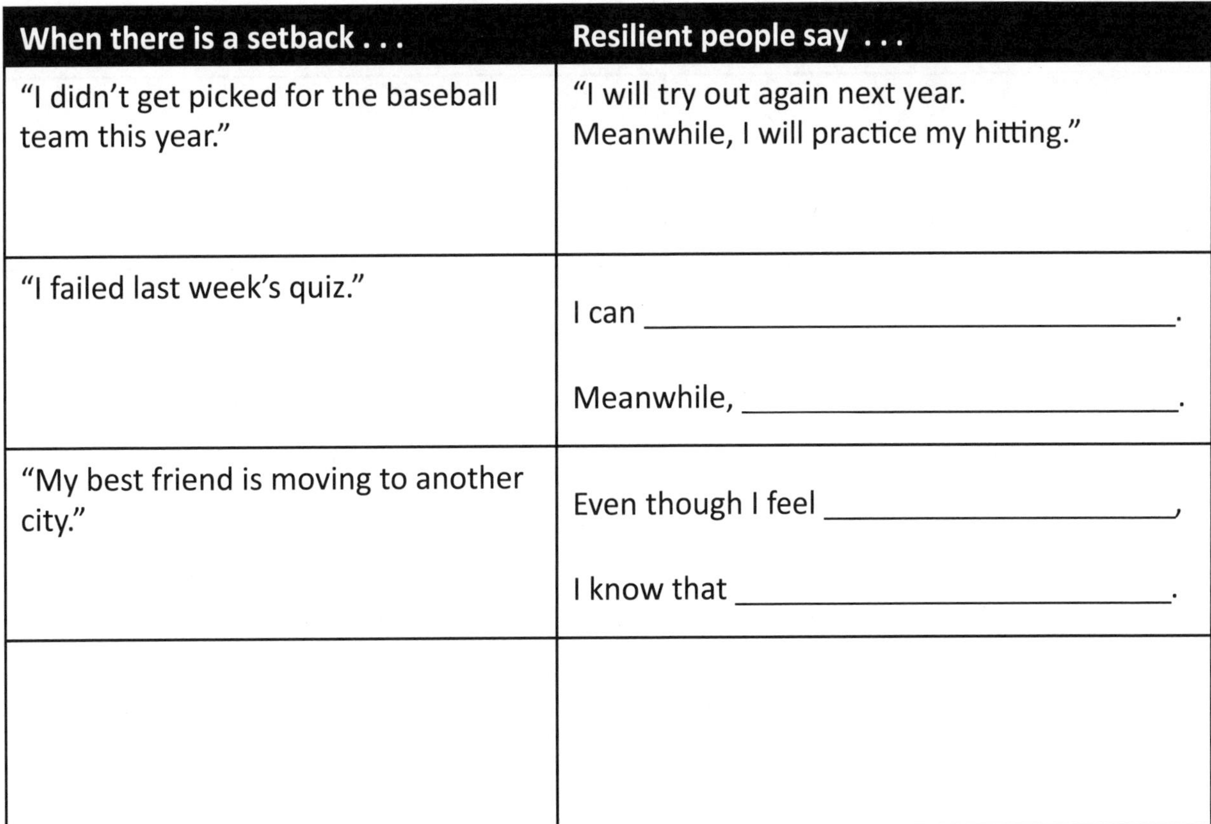

When there is a setback . . .	Resilient people say . . .
"I didn't get picked for the baseball team this year."	"I will try out again next year. Meanwhile, I will practice my hitting."
"I failed last week's quiz."	I can ____________________. Meanwhile, ____________________.
"My best friend is moving to another city."	Even though I feel ____________________, I know that ____________________.

Continued on next page

When there is a setback . . .	Resilient people say . . .

Explore the Science. Research shows that a good way to grow your resilience is to be around safe, caring adults. At home and at school, these are the people who want you to learn and grow. They don't protect you from every single problem. Instead, they teach you how to solve some problems yourself. They help you stay positive even when times are tough. Who are the safe, caring adults in your life?

Perseverance: Don't Give Up!

In your history lessons at school, you have probably read about men, women, and children who persevered in the struggle for Civil Rights. They faced difficulty after difficulty as they worked to achieve equality under the law, but they kept their "eyes on the prize."

For example, in 1960 Ruby Bridges was only six years old when she became the first black student to attend an all-white school. Many people had persevered so that Ruby could exercise her rights. But her need to persevere had only just begun.

First, she had to walk through an angry mob under police escort. Then, all but one teacher refused to teach her. Meanwhile, her father lost his job, and her grandparents were turned off the land that they had been farming—all because of other people's fear and ignorance.

What Is Perseverance? Ruby Bridges and her family refused to let anything stop them from achieving their goal. They faced each difficulty, day after day, to stand up for their civil rights. That willingness to face difficulties, delays, and other challenges in order to achieve a goal is called perseverance (pur-suh-VEER-ans). When you have perseverance, you don't give up. You use all your other grit traits and keep moving toward your goal.

Turn and Talk. Discuss some of the reasons that people persevere.

- To find freedom and opportunity
- To help solve problems in the world
- To overcome physical challenges

Continued on next page

Can you think of people you have met or read about who had perseverance? Share your ideas on the chart below.

Big goals or dreams that people seek to fulfill	Difficulties, delays, or discouragement they may face	What helps people persevere

Explore the Science. Professor John Gurdon is a Nobel Prize winner for his important work in biology, the science of living things. But when he was a boy, something happened that could have caused him to give up. A school-master wrote a discouraging note on young John's report card. Citing John's performance in school so far, the teacher wrote, "I believe he has ideas about becoming a scientist. On his present showing, this is quite ridiculous."

Instead of giving up, John decided to persevere. He worked hard and learned as much as he could about science. He even framed the schoolmaster's report! Today, he tells other scientists, "If experiments—or other things—do not succeed at once, don't give up!"

Apply the Trait. Write in your journal: What is your dream, or goal, in life? How long do you think it would take to achieve it? What challenges do you think you may face along the way? How could practicing some of the other grit traits help you persevere?

Hard Work: Give Your Best Effort

In stories about superheroes, the superhero has a special power that ordinary human beings don't have. For example, if a superhero wants to fly, he or she does it instantly. If a human being wants to fly (an airplane), he or she has to:

- Learn how to read, including maps
- Follow safety rules
- Study airplanes and the science of flight
- Take hundreds of hours of flying lessons
- Pass special tests

What Is Hard Work? Hard work means giving your time, attention, and effort in order to get a meaningful result. You may work hard to write a story so it will entertain people. You may work hard to care for a new pet so it will grow up healthy.

Even the things we most want to do can take work. When we are willing to work, it can lead to enjoyable experiences. From sports to entertainment, working with computers or helping people, there are many great ways to use your skills. They all take hard work.

Turn and Talk. Think of an interesting job you might like to do some day. With a partner, make a list of skills you will need for your jobs. Show some of the hard work it would take for you to do that job well. Start with work that you can do in school.

Continued on next page

Explore the Science. A scientist named Carol Dweck discovered something interesting about how people learn. She studied how students responded when solving math problems:

- Students with a fixed mindset had a negative view of hard work. They tried to avoid difficult questions, and, if they made a mistake, they felt discouraged or even bad about themselves.
- Students with a growth mindset made mistakes, too. However, they kept working hard. Instead of saying, "I can't do it," they said, "I can't do it yet" and tried again.

Guess which group made more progress in learning? Why?

____

____

____

____

____

____

Conscientiousness: Details Count!

Imagine that you have just finished writing a homework assignment that is due tomorrow. You worked hard to give thoughtful answers to each of the questions. Now you are done—or are you?

As you look at the paper, you notice that it is sort of messy. Maybe your handwriting is hard to read, or you made a few mistakes as you typed it on a computer.

What would you do?

Some students might turn it in anyway and "hope for the best." But gritty students know that it's better *to give the best effort*. They would take the time to type or write out the paper again so that it was clear, accurate, and easy to read.

What Is Conscientiousness? Conscientiousness is more than hard work. It means that when you work, you pay attention to the details. You make sure that your homework is neat, orderly, and organized. You do the work thoroughly—answering every question and following all directions.

Being conscientious does *not* mean you have to be perfect. For example, it would not be healthy to stay up all night writing and re-writing a paper. You need a good night's sleep in order to learn. Instead, you can work conscientiously by

- using all of your homework time,
- giving your best effort,
- checking directions,
- being neat, and
- turning your work in on time.

Often, being conscientious means taking just a little more time and care.

Continued on next page

Explore the Science. Imagine if you could predict someone's future, maybe even your own! Scientists say that they can tell how well students will do in school (and later, in life) by finding out how conscientious they are. In fact, conscientiousness is a better predictor of success than intelligence is.

Research shows that people who are conscientious are also likely to be curious. They ask questions, read a lot, and find out as much as they can. Conscientious people are almost never bored or careless.

Apply the Science. Make a list of topics you are curious about. Exchange lists with a partner and discuss one item each. Brainstorm five ways to find out more, then make a list. Is your list complete, specific, and well-organized?

Five Ways to Find Out More About ________________________________

1. ________________________________

____

2. ________________________________

____

3. ________________________________

____

4. ________________________________

____

5. ________________________________

____

Tenacity: Don't Let Go!

How long should you hold on to your goals? How long should you try? Just ask Diana Nyad, a long-distance swimmer. In her most famous achievement of all, Nyad became the first person to swim from Cuba to Florida without a shark cage—a distance of 110 miles!

So how did she do it? Tenacity! You see, Nyad had been swimming ever since she was a young woman. She also spent many years training for this achievement. She broke records and won awards on the way, but she never let go of her greatest goal of all.

On her first attempt, Nyad failed. She also failed on her second, third, and fourth attempts. Still, she held on to her goal. Determined as ever, Nyad tried again in 2013, and finally, on attempt number five, she succeeded. She was 64 years old.

What Is Tenacity? Tenacity is a way of holding on to things that you cannot see, such as ideas, goals, and efforts. For example, you can hold on to a promise to turn your homework in on time. You can hold on to a daily effort to improve your reading skills. No matter what challenges you face, when you use your tenacity, you don't let go.

People who have tenacity are gritty! They don't let short-term problems cause them to "drop the ball." They hold on in order to meet long-term goals. They learn to withstand challenges and setbacks.

Explore the Science. In "Why Academic Tenacity Matters," an article that first appeared in *Scientific American*, author Scott Barry Kaufman gives several more examples of ways that tenacious students hold on to their learning goals. Find the article and discuss it with your classmates. How many of the Top Ten Tenacity Behaviors can you practice as well?

Continued on next page

Turn and Talk. With a partner, talk about the examples below. Then add your own long-term goals and short-term challenges to the list. How will you use tenacity to move beyond the challenge and to hold on to your goal?

Long-term goal	Short-term challenge	My tenacity
Take part in the school spelling bee in two months.	There are 300 unfamiliar words on the spelling list.	I will practice 5 words a day, every morning, before I go to school.
Improve my skills by going to tutoring.	The tutoring starts early each Saturday morning.	Sleeping late is nice, but learning is more important, so I will hold on to my goal.

Social Intelligence: Be a Good Neighbor

Imagine that there are two beautiful parks in your neighborhood.

- In Park A, the kids say hi, take turns using the playground equipment, and invite others to join in their games. They listen to each other. If one of the littlest kids falls down or seems upset, the older kids help them.
- In Park B, no one really talks except to shout things like, "Me first!" and "Hey, that's mine!" There's a lot of activity, but no cooperation. If someone's feelings get hurt, it can quickly end up in a fight.

It's an easy choice to guess which park you'd prefer! While both groups of kids were probably smart, that is not the same as being socially intelligent.

What Is Social Intelligence? When you are socially intelligent, you get along well with others. You may be very outgoing or a little shy, but you understand "roles and rules." For example, as a member of a family, how do you respond when another family member asks you to help out? What are some of the ways you cooperate with others at school?

In everyday life, most people try to get along with others. In the "Two Parks" scenario you just read, imagine that the kids in Park B decide to resolve their conflicts. What are some rules and habits that would help them have a more positive experience? How could they use their social intelligence?

Explore the Science. Scientists like Daniel Goleman believe that "thinking and feeling go hand in hand in the classroom." Examples of this include:

- Considering how another student may be feeling
- Trying to understand someone's point of view in a class discussion
- Learning how to disagree politely
- Expressing your feelings without being controlled by them
- Thinking about your speech and actions, even when you feel upset

Continued on next page

Turn and Talk. With a partner, brainstorm at least three ways that your class practices social intelligence. Use the list below if you need help getting started.

Share your social intelligence ideas with the class. Your teacher can display them next to the classroom rules.

Ways Our Class Practices Social Intelligence:

We show respect for ____

____.

We listen actively by ____

____.

If someone feels upset, we ___________________________________

____.

We use positive words and phrases, like ________________________

____.

We cooperate when ____

____.

We share ____

____.

Grit Trait of the Week

Choose a grit trait and someone who has it. Make this award for that person. It might even be you!

WOW

THE GRIT TRAIT OF THE WEEK

awarded to

for

Grit traits: conscientiousness, courage, delayed gratification, gratitude, hard work, open-mindedness, optimism, perseverance, persistence, resilience, self-control, social intelligence, tenacity

My Grit Genealogy

Here's a great idea for people of all ages. Writing your Grit Genealogy is a bit like creating your family tree, but with a twist.

- A family tree shows the relationships between people in several generations of a family. Another word for family tree is *genealogy*.
- When you create your Grit Genealogy, you show how people in several generations of your family taught you about grit through their good example.

Where did you get your grit? Who are the people who helped you develop your character and your mindset? What were their grit traits? How did they teach you their virtues and values?

Trace your grit genealogy on the next page. Then practice the grit trait of gratitude. Write a message to thank those who have share their grit with you.

"If I have seen further it is that I have been standing on the shoulders of giants."

—Sir Isaac Newton

Thank You

____

____

____

____

____

Grit traits: conscientiousness, courage, delayed gratification, gratitude, hard work, open-mindedness, optimism, perseverance, persistence, resilience, self-control, social intelligence, tenacity

My Grit Genealogy

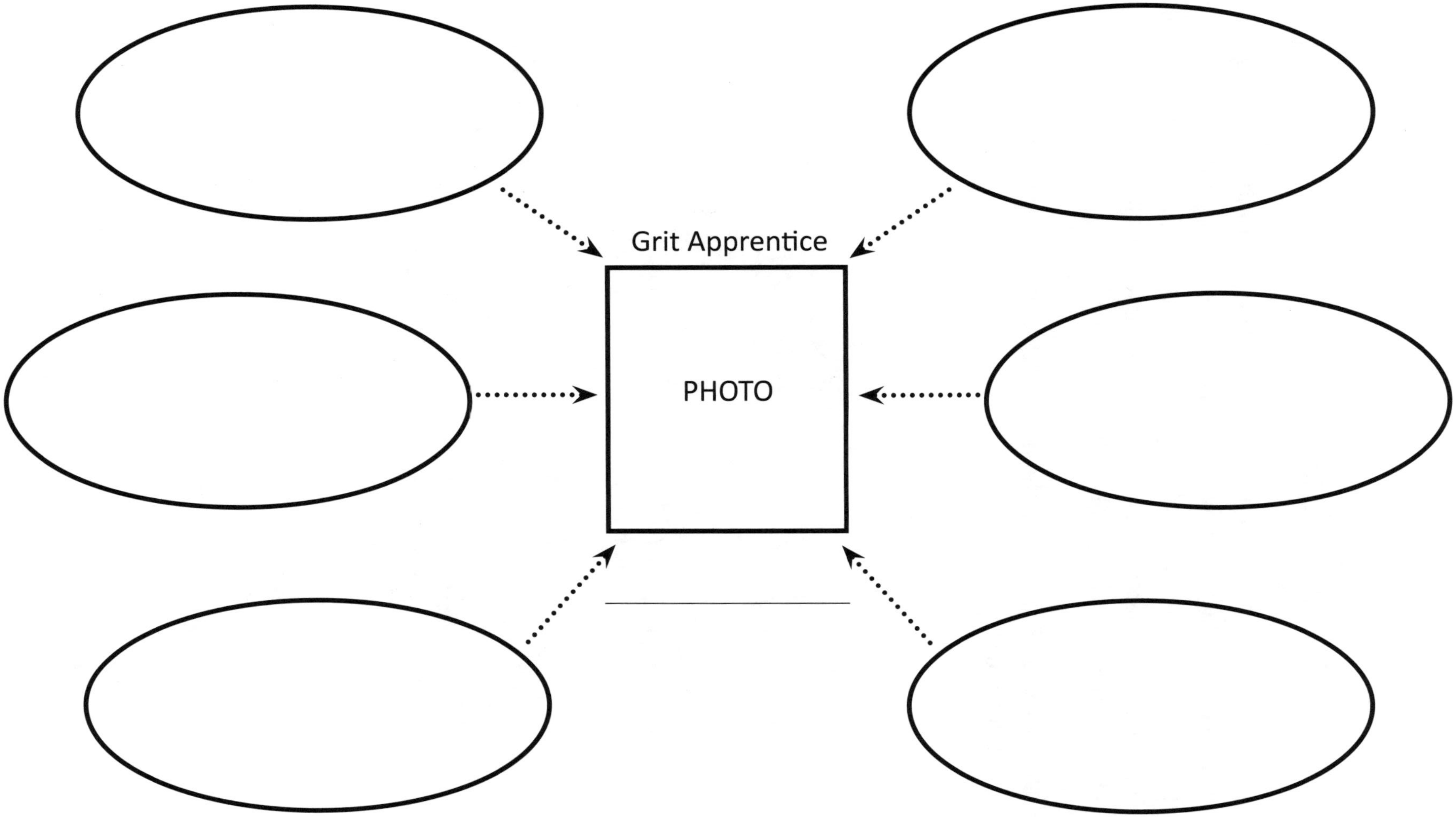

Grit Apprentice

PHOTO

Star Role Models

"Won't you be my neighbor?"
—Mr. Rogers

Some of the people in our lives are like stars because their shining example helps "light" our way. Just as stars are all around us in the night sky, be sure to surround yourself with Star Role Models. A Star Role Model can be a parent, grandparent, teacher, neighbor, or fellow classmate—anyone who has inspired you and helped you develop a growth mindset.

Who are your Star Role Models? Write their names around the star and tell about them.

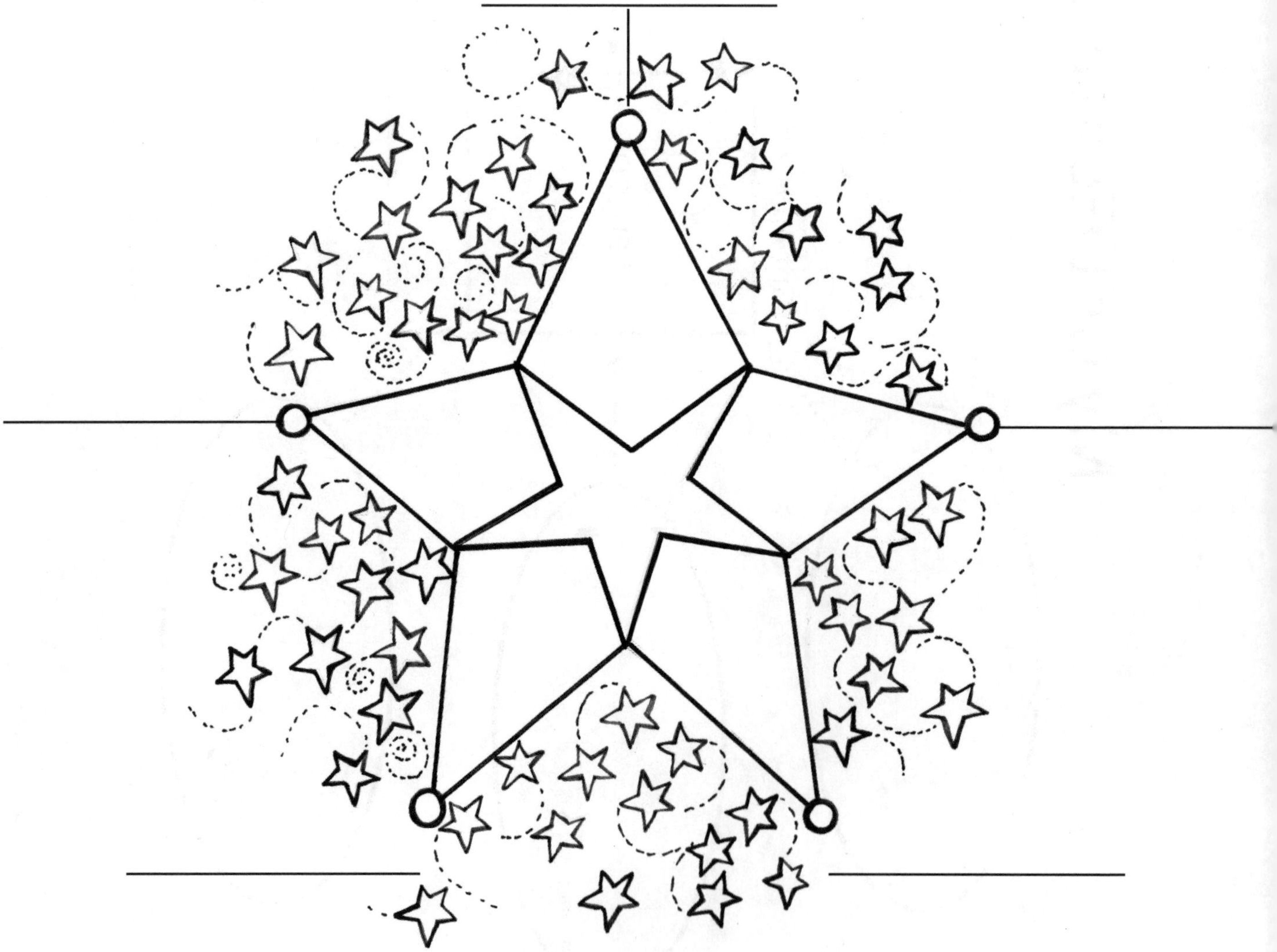

Courage Perseverance Optimism Open-Mindedness Self-Control Social Intelligence Gratitude

I've Got Grit

Complete the sentences to tell about your grit traits.

I've got grit because ____

____.

I use my grit traits to ____

____.

One of my grit traits is ____

____.

For example, ____

____.

Another of my grit traits is ____

____.

For example, ____

____.

Grit traits: conscientiousness, courage, delayed gratification, gratitude, hard work, open-mindedness, optimism, perseverance, persistence, resilience, self-control, social intelligence, tenacity

I Go for My Goals

Consider. In 2011, a scientist named Angela Duckworth led a study of middle school students. One group set goals for improving their math skills and made a plan for meeting those goals. The other group did not.

Discover. The students who set goals completed **60 percent** more practice questions during their break than the students who did not set goals. Why did the students who set goals work harder, even during their breaks?

Another researcher, Gabriele Oettingen, may have found the reason why. She learned that people report feeling more "energized" when they

- Decide what goal they WISH to achieve
- Imagine the best possible OUTCOME
- Write down the OBSTACLES, and
- PLAN the specific steps they will take.

Oettingen calls her strategy W-O-O-P.

Turn and Talk. With a partner, talk over these questions:

- What goal do you wish to achieve?
- What positive outcome do you picture?
- What obstacles do you face?
- What steps do you plan to take?

Go for Your Goal. When you are ready, write about your goal in more detail. You can also make a poster to go with your goal, using the ideas on Resource 59.

Grit traits: conscientiousness, courage, delayed gratification, gratitude, hard work, open-mindedness, optimism, perseverance, persistence, resilience, self-control, social intelligence, tenacity

MY GOAL

How do you want to grow, or improve, in your learning?

____

____

____

THE OUTCOME I WANT

Imagine you have achieved your goal. Picture it. Write about it. Use details.

"There is always a step small enough from where we are to get us to where we want to be. If we take that small step, there's always another we can take, and eventually a goal thought to be too far to reach becomes achievable."

—Ellen Langer

"Picture your brain forming new connections as you meet the challenge and learn. Keep on going."

—Carol Dweck

Continued on next page

MY OBSTACLES

What obstacles do you face? What obstacles do you feel inside?

____

____

____

MY PLAN

What steps can you take? Make a list. Be as specific as you can.

I will start from a growth mindset because I ____________________.

If ____________________, then I will ____________________.

If ____________________, then I will ____________________.

If ____________________, then I will ____________________.

I can use my grit traits, too:

I have ____________________, so I can ____________________.

I have ____________________, so I can ____________________.

I have ____________________, so I can ____________________.

Even if ____________________,

I will keep going because ____________________.

Turn your goal into art.

Keep it where you can see it every day.

Goal (what I want to do):

____

____

____

Reason (why it will benefit me):

____

____

____

Obstacle (where I might get stuck):

____

____

____

Work (what I plan to do):

____

____

____

Optimism: Positive People in My Grit Corner

Have you ever noticed that people who are optimistic seem to have more energy? Positive people also seem to spread that energy whenever you're around them. After all, it feels better to be around people who mostly smile, laugh, and share kindness than it does to be around people who mostly frown, complain, and say negative things.

> *"Surround yourself with the dreamers and the doers, the believers and the thinkers, but most of all, surround yourself with those who see the greatness within you, even when you don't see it yourself."* —Edmund Lee

List the Optimistic People You Know. These are the people who are "in your corner" because they are a positive influence in your life. You might even say that they're in your "Grit Corner"!

"A pessimist sees the difficulty in every opportunity; an optimist sees the opportunity in every difficulty"
– Sir Winston Churchill

MY GRIT CORNER—Optimistic People in My Life

1.

2.

3.

4.

5.

Turn and Talk. With a partner, take turns sharing about one or two of the Optimistic People on your list. Tell why they inspire you to be optimistic, too.

Optimism: I Practice Positive Self–Talk

Positive self-talk is the one of the most effective strategies you can use to strengthen your perseverance. Practice positive self-talk as a way to grow your courage and keep up a growth mindset. This will also help you rid yourself of any self-defeating thoughts. For example: I'm a steady worker and I always keep up with my assignments.

"Every time you state what you want or believe, you're the first to hear it. It's a message to both you and others about what you think is possible. Don't put a ceiling on yourself."

—Oprah Winfrey

POSITIVE SELF-TALK

1.

2.

3.

4.

5.

6.

7.

Grit traits: conscientiousness, courage, delayed gratification, gratitude, hard work, open-mindedness, optimism, perseverance, persistence, resilience, self-control, social intelligence, tenacity

My Attitude of Gratitude

Practicing gratitude is a great way to grow your grit. When you make a daily habit of appreciating what you are thankful for in life, your attitude becomes more and more positive. Even on challenging days, you start to pay more attention to the positive and to tune out the negative.

This, in turn, has a way of leading to more reasons for gratitude. People with an attitude of gratitude focus on the positive and look for the good in people. This lowers stress and helps them make better choices.

Practice gratitude every day so it becomes part of who you are. Here's how:

- With your class, brainstorm groups of people in your community who deserve a thank-you note or video. For example, you may be grateful for your area's firefighters, librarians, or volunteers. Find out more about one of the groups. Then write to that group as a class.
- With a partner or group, describe people or things you are grateful for.
- In a journal, list "Three Reasons I Am Grateful Right Now." Consider adding three reasons every day for one week, or even one month.

  Start by listing three reasons here.

"When eating fruit, think of the person who planted the seed."

—Anonymous

1. ______________________________

____

2. ______________________________

____

3. ______________________________

____

I Practice Persistence

Materials: Paper or poster board, color markers

Summary. Most people are more creative than they give themselves credit for. Here is a great whole-class activity that will show your students how "grit" can help them be even more creative.

Practice Persistence. First, invite groups of students to make lists of ideas. For example, each group can generate a list for one of the following:

- Ideas for healthy lunchbox snacks
- Kinds of animals
- Types of outdoor activities

Next, ask students to raise their hands when their group has run out of ideas. When all groups have raised their hands, say: *Let's try something new. Instead of giving up, let's keep going for just two more minutes. How many ideas do you think your group can come up with in two more minutes?* Record the estimates.

Have students use a new color to add to their lists. When time is up, invite students to count how many ideas they came up with when they persisted.

Share the Science. Researchers at Northwestern University report that people underestimate how many creative ideas they can think up if they keep going instead of giving up. In one study, people were asked to generate a list of word associations and then given a few minutes break.

Prior to the break, they were asked to estimate how many more ideas they could add to their lists. Most participants estimated that they could only add a few more ideas. After the break, participants were asked to add to their lists. The majority of participants generated more ideas than they had estimated they would.

Guide students to recognize that by being persistent they can achieve more, be more creative, and become better learners.

Persistence: Word Play

"Mrs. Lessard, you misunderheard me"

—Seth Johnson

Have fun while you strengthen your grit traits. Make up new words by combining words you learn about grit to invent words of your own.

Here are some examples:

- You can blend the words *Grit* and *Integrity* to create the word *Gritegrity*, "the capacity to always do the right thing."
- You can blend the words *Optimism* and *Tenacity* to create the word *Optiminacity*, "a positive determination to hold fast to something important, such as a goal."

How Many Words Can You Blend? Practice the grit trait Persistence as you form new words. Challenge yourself to come up with at least three new words. Then see if you can persist in adding a few more.

My New Grit Words

Grit	+	Integrity	=	Gritegrity
Optimism	+	Tenacity	=	Optiminacity
______	+	______	=	______
______	+	______	=	______
______	+	______	=	______
______	+	______	=	______
______	+	______	=	______
______	+	______	=	______

I Overcome Obstacles

Recall a time when you overcame obstacles. How did your grit traits help you face the challenge?

"If you can't fly, then run; if you can't run, then walk; if you can't walk, then crawl; but whatever you do, you have to keep moving forward."

—Martin Luther King, Jr.

My challenge:

Why this was a challenge to me:

What I did:

What changed:

What I learned from facing my challenge:

Grit traits: conscientiousness, courage, delayed gratification, gratitude, hard work, open-mindedness, optimism, perseverance, persistence, resilience, self-control, social intelligence, tenacity

I Bounce Back from Setbacks

Thomas Edison did not succeed at his first attempt to develop a light bulb. In fact, it took him at least 1,000 times before he was successful. When a reporter asked him, "How did it feel to fail **1,000 times**?" Edison replied, "I didn't fail **1,000 times**. The light bulb was an invention with **1,000 steps**."

Read more about Thomas Edison or another famous person you admire. As you do, use a T chart like this one to track their setbacks and their progress. You can also use the T chart to track your own setbacks and progress.

Setbacks	Progress

Goals: Know When to Change Horses

Perseverance is surely one of the greatest virtues among the grit traits. However, this doesn't mean you should keep doing something that clearly cannot work. As the old saying shows, sometimes sticking with the same plan, action, or approach is like riding a dead horse—it's just not going to take you anywhere. When that happens, it's important to try something new.

So how do you know when to keep trying and when to "change horses"?

First. Seek advice from a teacher or other caring adult. Share your goal and the steps you are taking to reach it. Then talk over questions like these.

- How much time have you already spent on this goal?

___

- How much personal effort have you been making?

___

___

- What have been your results so far?

___

___

- How are you feeling about your efforts? Do you feel mostly optimistic or do you feel mostly frustrated or "stuck"?

___

___

___

"If you're riding a horse and it dies, get off"

—attributed to ancient Dakota tribal wisdom

Continued on next page

Next. Decide what needs to change.

- Is your goal realistic? Do you truly care about achieving your goal? If not, you can change your goal.

  ____

  ____

  ____

- Is there a better way? If so, you can change your plan, or one or more of the steps.

  ____

  ____

  ____

Then. Use your grit traits to help you through this process, too!

Which grit traits will help you . . .

- bounce back from any feelings of disappointment or frustration?

  ____

- stay open to new ways of meeting your goals?

  ____

- work patiently with the new plan?

  ____

- thank the adult who helped you talk over your new plan?

  ____

I Can Self-Regulate

It takes grit to meet a learning challenge. But what do you do if a challenge causes stress? Here's a guide to some helpful strategies you can use. Brainstorm with your partner to add ideas of your own.

When I feel . . .	I can . . .
Distracted	• Take notes or draw a mind map to help me record important ideas. • Check my posture to make sure that I am sitting comfortably but not slouching. • Look at the person who is speaking. • __________ • __________
Frustrated or upset	• Breathe in slowly and slowly breathe out. Repeat this three times. • If I still feel upset, I can write or draw to show why. I can share this with my teacher. • __________ • __________
Confused	• Ask questions. • Talk with a partner to check understanding. • Reread. List and look up unfamiliar words. • __________ • __________
Stuck	• Put my hands on my desk, relax my shoulders, and sit quietly for about 30 seconds. • Picture the problem in my mind as if I am seeing it for the first time. • __________ • __________

I Have Sisu

> *"Sisu, a word from Finland, means strength of will, determination, and perseverance in the face of adversity . . . the ability to persist after most people would quit and to keep on trying, with the will to win."*
>
> —Anonymous

Create or find your own Sisu symbol. This is something that can remind you of your courage, perseverance, and resilience—the grit traits you need in order to take action during difficult times. It may be

- a photo in a magazine,
- a line from a poem that you can illustrate, or
- a picture of a favorite statue or person from history.

Describe your Sisu symbol. Display it where you can see it every day.

Start with the Difficult Part

Jot down a few notes about how you do your homework.

- Which assignment do you usually do first?

 ____

- Which assignment do you usually do last?

 ____

- Why do you do the assignments in this order?

 ____

When you answer questions for homework, what order do you follow? Underline one response:

- I do each question in order.
- I skip the hardest questions and come back to them later.
- I do the hardest questions first before I move on to others.
- I only do the questions that I know how to answer.

Turn and Talk. Share your responses with a partner. Do you do the hardest assignments or questions first, last, or in order? Why do you think that is? It's human to feel like choosing do what seems the easiest thing first. But sometimes doing the hard part first can make everything easier and more enjoyable.

To understand why, just think about how you feel when you are avoiding the hard part of a task. Chances are, you are worrying about it, or feeling dislike about having to do it. All that negative thinking seems to build up in the back of your mind. It takes energy from you and makes it difficult to focus. It can also make the task that you are avoiding seem bigger and more complicated than it really is.

Continued on next page

Try This Strategy. Many people have reported that when they do the most difficult task first, it gives them a feeling of accomplishment or makes them feel energized and inspired. Some people are surprised to discover that the task that they were avoiding turned out to be much easier than they had expected! Now what might happen if you and your partner each try doing the difficult part first?

Practice the Strategy. With your partner, agree to try doing a difficult question, assignment, or task first. This could be work that you do in class or at home. Later, compare your work and talk about the experience. How did it feel to do the difficult part first?

___

___

___

How did it affect how you felt as you moved on to the easier part of your work?

___

___

___

___

What Would Your Superhero Do?

"A hero is an ordinary individual who finds the strength to persevere and endure in spite of overwhelming obstacles."

—Christopher Reeve

The late actor Christopher Reeve was well known for his portrayal of the onscreen hero, Superman. When Reeve was paralyzed as the result of an accident, it put an end to his movie career. However, through his courage and other grit traits, he became a real-life superhero, as he spoke up on behalf of people with spinal-cord injuries.

Who are your superheroes?

1.

2.

3.

What do your superheroes do?

____

____

____

What would your superhero say about you?

____

____

____

Here's My Grit Card

Create and share baseball-style Grit Cards to trade with your classmates. Use a glue stick to add a current photograph to the original card. Next, add details to let others know not only who you are, but what you value. Then, photocopy your cards, trade them, and see how many cards you can collect. (Be sure to keep a copy of your own card!)

My Daily "Grituals"

Daily grit-building rituals—"grituals"—are practices that you build into your day. They are not ordinary habits, actions that you do over and over again without any real thought. Instead, they are positive habits that you first think about carefully, plan in detail, and then practice to help you make a positive change.

For example, an ordinary habit might be buttoning up your coat or putting on your socks. That's something you have already done hundreds of times and which you don't really think about.

A gritual, on the other hand, can help you start the day with a positive mind-set or practice one of your grit traits. For example, you might commit to:

- Practicing positive self-talk for a minute every morning
- Spending five minutes every evening writing reasons for gratitude into your journal
- Doing a physical activity before you turn on any computer devices
- Checking your backpack before and after school
- Raising your hand in class more often
- Taking a step—or micro-step—toward one of your goals every day

____

____

____

Continued on next page

My Daily Gritual

Choose one of the ideas on the previous page or create a gritual of your own. Be as specific as you can about what you are going to do.

____

____

____

____

____

Use this space to picture your gritual.

As you practice your daily gritual, it will give your growth mindset a boost and make it easier for you to set and achieve goals. It will also help you build your character, as you will become more dependable—to yourself as well as to others!

5
Creatively Gritty

When art imitates grit, students can integrate inspiration!

Grit Cloud: Seeking Word Power

"Without knowing the force of words, it is impossible to know more."
—Confucius

Create your own grit word cloud. Here's how:

1. Using a computer, copy a text that you have read or written about grit traits.
2. Go to Wordle.net, or another online word-cloud generator. (Be sure to follow your school's rules about using the Internet.)
3. Paste the text into the online text box and click "Go" (or "Submit").

The words will appear in a new form, called a word cloud.

The bigger the size of the words, the more times that word occurs in your text. The size may also indicate which grit words are most important to you.

Select one or two words from your grit cloud to focus on each week. Practice making these grit traits part of your character.

resilience
failure
quality learned
greatest
mind learning absence
afraid triumph next
storms continue over anything
ship fear without
sail honor
Success effort never
optimism world counts
final
courage

Daily Grit Reminder

From Happier to Grittier. A recent study at Northwestern University studied people who received a brief daily message that reminded them to make choices that would help promote happiness.

At the end of a week, the people who received reminders reported feeling happier than people who did not receive the reminder. Why not apply this science to the concept of grittiness?

Make Daily Reminders. You can make Daily Grit Reminders like the one below.

- Fill in the grit trait that you want the student(s) to practice during the designated period.
- Distribute the reminders every day for one to two weeks.
- At the end of that period, ask volunteers to share the effect of the daily reminder on their experiences with the particular grit trait.

Your Daily Grit Reminder

Dear Student,

This is a gentle reminder to practice your grit traits today,

especially ______________________________.

Please take a moment to recall what you have learned about this trait.

Remember, the more you practice your grit traits, the better you will become at making good choices and progressing toward your goals.

Have a great and gritty day!

Sincerely,

____

Morning Message-Meister

Do you have an inspiring statement that you would like to share with others? You and your classmates can take turns volunteering as Morning Message-Meister. It's a great way to help set a positive tone at the first assembly or class meeting of the day.

"My life is my message"
—Mahatma Gandhi

To get started, find or write one or two sentences about one of these topics:

- Grit in general, or a specific grit trait, such as optimism, persistence, or conscientiousness
- The importance of a having a growth mindset
- A value, virtue, or character trait, such as honesty, fairness, or respect

Some great sources of messages include:

- Stories about fictional characters. Notice what they say and what others say about them.
- News articles, biographies, and history selections. Notice how people act and how it affects others.
- Quotations that you find online, on posters, and in special books of quotations from your school or public library. Think about why a certain quotation inspires you and why you think it will inspire others.

You may find it helpful to share and discuss your quotation with a teacher or a classmate. This will give you a chance to make any edits and to practice any comment you would like to share with the class about why you chose that quotation. Ask yourself how your Morning Message will help or inspire others.

____

____

____

____

Change the Story

Read this story on your own or with a partner. Then use what you've learned about a growth mindset to change the story for the better.

"I'm Just Not a Good Speller"

The problem. Jon did not do well on his spelling test. "I'm just not a good speller," he told himself. "If I were smart, I would already know how to spell every word correctly. I would never make mistakes."

But is that really true? Here's what happened:

Two days before the spelling test, Jon took out the word list and stared at it. "I don't remember what some of these words mean," he said. He put the list away.

The next morning at school, one of Jon's classmates asked if he wanted to practice for the spelling test.

"No way!" said Jon. "Do you think I'm stupid? Smart people don't need to practice."

That afternoon, the class brainstormed strategies for learning spelling words. Jon stared out the window. Then he took out a notebook and a pen. He made doodles all over the page. He had questions but didn't want to look dumb.

After school, Jon started to do his homework. He was supposed to write sentences using some of the spelling words. What he wanted to do was play video games.

"I'll play just one game first and then do my homework." But it was so much fun that he lost track of time. Soon it was suppertime, then bedtime. That night Jon had trouble sleeping.

Continued on next page

Jon was late for school the next morning. He had skipped breakfast and had to run all the way because he missed the bus. When he got to class, the spelling test had already started. He had missed two questions.

At least he heard the other questions. However, he only answered the easy questions. He didn't want to make any mistakes. Besides, he was bored.

So Jon did not do well. His teacher said to the class, "For your next spelling test, I will include several words from the last test. So if you missed any of those words, you have another chance to try again."

"What's the point?" thought Jon. "There's nothing I can do to change things. I'm just not good at spelling."

Change the Story

Get Ready. Think about Jon's story.

Talk About It.

- Right now Jon is stuck in a fixed mindset, but he can develop a growth mindset. *What if he changes the way he talks to himself and others?*
- Right now Jon believes there is nothing he can do to improve. *What kind of actions can Jon take? What strategies can he use?*
- What are some traits that would be helpful to Jon? For example, think about how it might it help him to:
  - Delay gratification (take care of more important things first)
  - Be optimistic
  - Show perseverance
- What could Jon have done to find out what the spelling words meant?
- What do you think of Jon's comments?
- What are some things that Jon could have done instead?

Work Together. Now work with your group to change Jon's story for the better.

Record. Make a list of your ideas. If you have time, write a few new paragraphs to show what Jon can do next.

Share. Ask someone in your group to report your ideas or read your story to the class. Invite the rest of the class to share their ideas.

Grit traits: conscientiousness, courage, delayed gratification, gratitude, hard work, open-mindedness, optimism, perseverance, persistence, resilience, self-control, social intelligence, tenacity

CAN-DO Card Game

Materials: Copy of the resource pages, index cards, glue sticks, scissors

With a partner, play a card game to practice turning fixed-mindset statements into growth-mindset statements. To make the playing cards, cut and paste the labels onto the backs of index cards.

To Play:

1. To start the game, put three Frown cards face up on the table.
2. Mix up the other cards and put them in one pile face down.
3. Take turns picking a card.
4. Does your card have a Frown? Set it on the table with the others.
5. Does your card have a Smile? Cover up a Frown card.

Keep playing until all the Frown cards have been covered by a Smile card!

You can also add to the game by making Frown and Smile cards of your own.

I can't do it.

I'm no good at that.

I'll never understand.

This is too hard.

I'm afraid to ake a mistake.

I can't make this any better.

I'll never get better at this.

I give up.

My plan failed.

____

____

____

____

____

____

____

____

____

____

____

____

____

____

I can do it.

I can ask questions.

I can get better.

I can work hard.

I can use a strategy I've learned.

I can always start over.

I can practice every day.

I can learn from my mistakes.

I can make a new plan.

____

____

____

____

____

____

____

____

____

____

____

____

____

____

My Six-Word Slogan

"I'm Stronger Than I've Ever Imagined"
——Marsha Wheatley

Describe yourself using only six words that tell about grit or the growth mindset. Start by looking at the Word Bank below. What other words and ideas come to mind?

You may find it challenging at first, so take your time. It is sometimes harder to write something short, when every word counts, than it is to write something lengthy.

Here are some Six-Word Slogans to help you get started.

- I Was Born To Be Gritty.
- I Know That I Can Grow!
- I'm Strong. I Never Give Up!
- "Can't" Isn't In My Word Bank!

effort	hard work	self-control
fortitude	ambition	resilience
nerve	resolve	open-mindedness
backbone	social agility	integrity
courage	enthusiasm	gratitude
determination	zest	volition
self-confidence	tenacity	optimism
initiative	perseverance	patience
curiosity	focus	self-confidence
honesty	persistence	empathy
social intelligence	optimism	commitment
goal-mindedness	reliability	willpower

Class Grit Flag

"Show what you believe in. Show what you are made of."—Anonymous

Work Collaboratively. Have students work collaboratively to create an inspirational Class Grit Flag. After students have had an opportunity to brainstorm, you may wish to have them come up with a few sample sketches. Students can then vote on which flag design to adopt as the class flag.

Remind students to include words or images that send a message about grit or the growth mindset. Some examples might include:

- An acorn and an oak tree
- The school mascot and a grit-trait word
- A phrase from a school song or cheer

Tip:

If students offer several excellent ideas for flags, you can extend the project by making a paper wall quilt for a school corridor.

Display the Flag. Students can also incorporate other elements, such as the school colors, and its vision or mission statement. Have students display the flag and explain its meaning to another class.

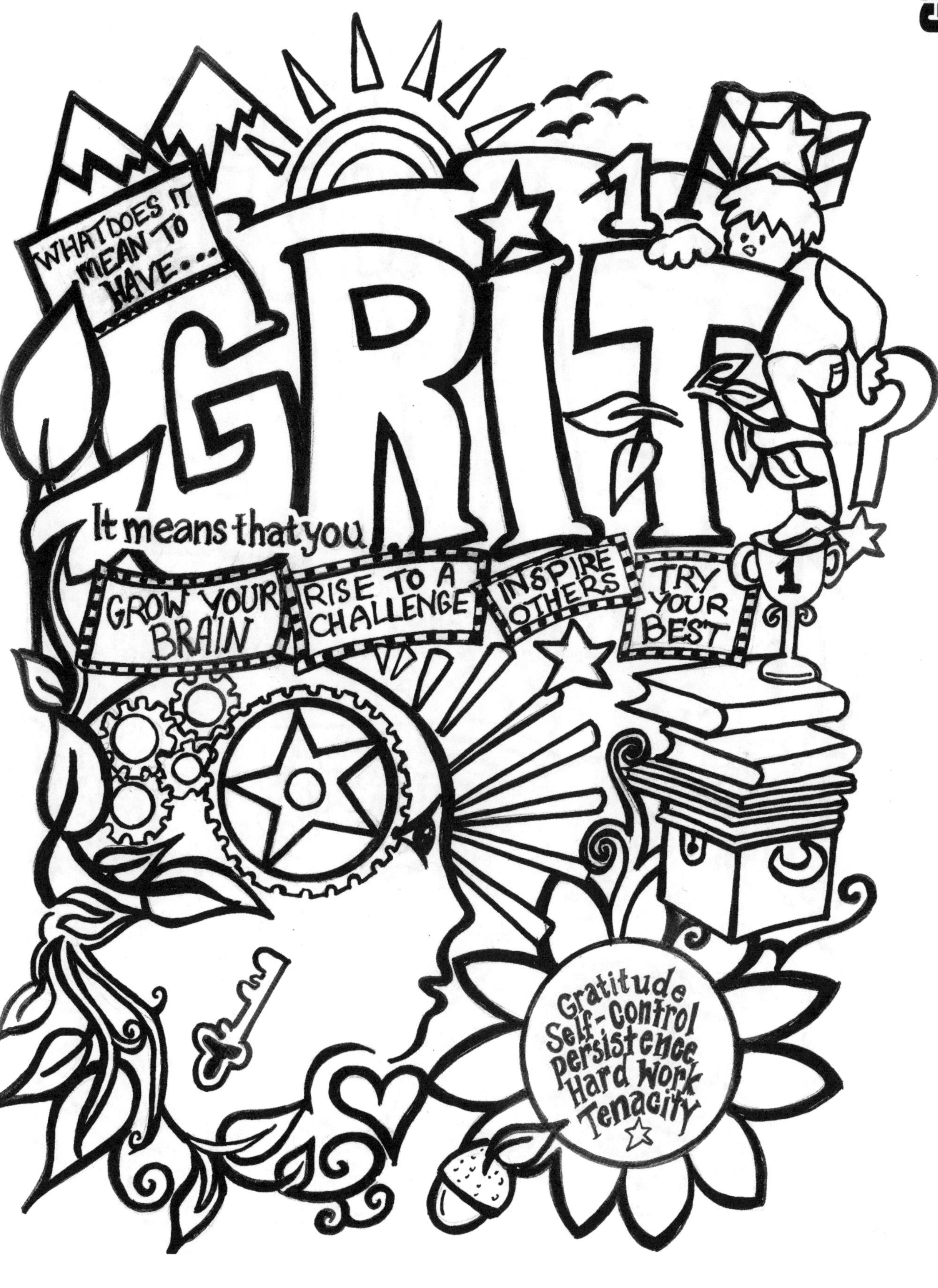

WHAT DOES IT MEAN TO HAVE...

GRIT

It means that you

GROW YOUR BRAIN

RISE TO A CHALLENGE

INSPIRE OTHERS

TRY YOUR BEST

Gratitude
Self-Control
persistence
Hard Work
Tenacity

DON'T BE AFRAID TO FAIL
It simply means that you have made your
FIRST ATTEMPT AT LEARNING
How many more attempts at learning am I allowed to make?
To get the answer... count the stars and multiply by 10
GRIT

Make Inspirational Posters

Make a poster to illustrate an inspiring quotation, and then share it with the class. You can find good quotations almost anywhere, including:

- In stories and interviews, songs and poems—Copy your favorite lines into a notebook.
- In quote books that list famous quotations by topic—You will find these at the library.
- Online at sites approved by your school—See if you can look up a grit trait and find a quotation about it.

You can also use one of these quotations:

- **You're right! Whether you think you can or think you can't, you're right.** *—Henry Ford*
- **The future belongs to those who believe in the beauty of their dreams.** *—Eleanor Roosevelt*
- **Do the best you can until you know better. Then when you know better, do better.** *—Maya Angelou*
- **In America, nobody says you have to keep the circumstances somebody else gives you.** *—Amy Tan*
- **I am only one, but still I am one. I cannot do everything, but still I can do something. And because I cannot do everything, I will not refuse to do the something that I can do.** *—Helen Keller*
- **Nothing great was ever achieved without enthusiasm.** *—Ralph Waldo Emerson*
- **The ones who are crazy enough to think they can change the world are the ones who do.** *—Steve Jobs*
- **If you are not willing to learn, no one can help you. If you are determined to learn, no one can stop you.** *—Zig Ziglar*

Make Inspirational Posters

[illegible]

6
Additional Grit Resources

And the grit goes on . . .

Glossary of Quotations

Character

Before I can live with other folks, I've got to live with myself. The one thing that doesn't abide by majority rule is a person's conscience.
—Atticus Finch in the novel To Kill a Mockingbird *by Harper Lee*

Courage

You will never do anything in this world without courage. It is the greatest quality of the mind next to honor.*—Aristotle*

I am not afraid of storms, for I am learning how to sail my ship.
—Louisa May Alcott

I learned that courage was not the absence of fear, but the triumph over it. *—Nelson Mandela*

Either you decide to stay in the shallow end of the pool or you go out in the ocean. *—Christopher Reeve*

Success is not final; failure is not fatal: It is the courage to continue that counts. *—Winston Churchill*

Fearless is getting back up and fighting for what you want over and over again...even though every time you've tried before you've lost. *—Taylor Swift*

Determination

"I can't" are two words that have never been in my vocabulary. I believe in me more than anything in this world. *—Wilma Rudolph*

Effort

You're not obligated to win. You're obligated to keep trying to do the best you can every day. *—Marian Wright Edelman*

I've always believed that if you put in the work, the results will come. I don't do things half-heartedly. Because I know if I do, then I can expect half-hearted results. *—Michael Jordan*

Gratitude

At times our own light goes out and is rekindled by a spark from another person. Each of us has cause to think with deep gratitude of those who have lighted the flame within us. *—Albert Schweitzer*

Gratitude is the sign of noble souls. *—Aesop*

Growth mindset

Since new developments are the products of a creative mind, we must therefore stimulate and encourage that type of mind in every way possible. *—George Washington Carver*

Nothing is impossible. The word itself says, "I'm possible!" *—Katherine Hepburn*

Write this down: "My life is full of unlimited possibilities."*—Pablo Valle*

Habit

Excellence is an art won by training and habituation. We do not act rightly because we have virtue or excellence, but we rather have those because we have acted rightly. We are what we repeatedly do. Excellence, then, is not an act but a habit. *—Aristotle*

Hard Work

Nothing will work unless you do. *—Maya Angelou*

A dream doesn't become reality through magic; it takes sweat, determination, and hard work. *—Colin Powell*

My parents didn't believe in luck. They believed in hard work and preparing me to take advantage of opportunity. *—Naveen Jain*

Talent is cheaper than table salt. What separates the talented individual from the successful one is a lot of hard work. *—Stephen King*

Power means happiness; power means hard work and sacrifice.
—Beyoncé Knowles

We all naturally want to become successful...we also want to take shortcuts. And it's easy to do so, but you can never take away the effort of hard work and discipline and sacrifice. *—Apollo Ohno*

Mistakes

I have missed more than 9,000 shots in my career. I have lost almost 300 games. On 26 occasions I have been entrusted to take the game-winning shot...and I missed. I have failed over and over and over again in my life. And that's precisely why I succeed. *—Michael Jordan*

Anyone who has never made mistakes has never tried anything new.
—Albert Einstein

Open-mindedness

If you want something you've never had, then you've got to do something you've never done. *—Anonymous*

Keep an open mind and a compassionate heart. *—Unknown*

You are confined only by the walls you build yourself. *—Unknown*

In most situations I am the problem. My mentalities, my pictures, my experiences form the biggest obstacles to my success.
—James A. Belasco, in Flight of The Buffalo

Optimism

Optimism is the faith that leads to achievement. *—Helen Keller*

Perpetual optimism is a force multiplier. *—Colin Powell*

I have never had to face anything that could overwhelm the native optimism and stubborn perseverance I was blessed with. *—Sonia Sotomayor*

A bad attitude is like a flat tire; you can't go anywhere until you change it. *—Unknown*

Perseverance

Most of the time I liked school and got good grades. In junior high, though, I hit a stumbling block with math—I used to come home and cry because of how frustrated I was! But after a few good teachers and a lot of perseverance, I ended up loving math and even choosing it as a major when I got to college. *—Danica McKellar*

Every person who has grown to any degree of usefulness, every person who has grown to distinction, almost without exception has been a person who has risen by overcoming obstacles, by removing difficulties, by resolving that when he met discouragement he would not give up. *—Booker T. Washington*

What everyone in the astronaut corps shares in common is not gender or ethnic background, but motivation, perseverance, and desire—the desire to participate in a voyage of discovery. *—Ellen Ochoa*

Persistence

Energy and persistence conquer all things. *—Benjamin Franklin*

Our greatest weakness lies in giving up. The most certain way to succeed is always to try just one more time. *—Thomas Edison*

The impatient idealist says: "Give me a place to stand and I shall move the earth." But such a place does not exist. We all have to stand on the earth itself and go with her at her pace. —*Chinua Achebe*

You have to apply yourself each day to becoming a little better. By applying yourself to the task of becoming a little better each and every day over a period of time, you will become a lot better. —*John Wooden*

Positive self-talk

I'm never going to put boundaries on myself ever again. I'm never going to say, "I can't do it." I'm never going to say, "Maybe." I'm never going to say, "I don't think I can." I can and I will." —*Nadiya Jamir Hussain*

Every time you state what you want or believe, you're the first to hear it. It's a message to both you and others about what you think is possible. Don't put a ceiling on yourself. —*Oprah Winfrey*

Don't bring negative to my door. —*Maya Angelou*

Resilience

Obstacles, of course, are developmentally necessary: they teach kids strategy, patience, critical thinking, resilience, and resourcefulness. —*Naomi Wolf*

However long the night, the dawn will break. —*African proverb*

Do not judge me by successes. Judge me by how many times I fell down and got up again. —*Nelson Mandela*

Persistence and resilience only come from having been given the chance to work through difficult problems. —*Gever Tulley*

If you don't like something, change it. If you can't change it, change your attitude. —*Maya Angelou*

Self-control

What lies in our power to do, lies in our power not to do. *—Aristotle*

I am, indeed, a king because I know how to rule myself. *—Pietro Aretino*

I am no bird; and no net ensnares me: I am a free human being with an independent will. *—Charlotte Brontë*

Tenacity

Let me tell you the secret that has led me to my goal. My strength lies solely in my tenacity. *—Louis Pasteur*

Tenacity is the ability to hang on when letting go appears most attractive. *—Unknown*

Often, it is tenacity, not talent, that rules the day. *—Julia Cameron*

Most of the things worth doing in the world had been declared impossible before they were done. *—Louis D. Brandeis*

Virtue

Virtue can only flourish among equals. *—Mary Wollstonecraft*

To practice five things under all circumstances constitutes perfect virtue; these five are gravity, generosity of soul, sincerity, earnestness, and kindness. *—Confucius*

True courage is not the brutal force of vulgar heroes, but the firm resolve of virtue and reason. *—Alfred North Whitehead*

I hope I shall possess firmness and virtue enough to maintain what I consider the most enviable of all titles, the character of an honest man. *—George Washington*

The Good Grit Reading List

Here are our recommendations for exploring grit traits in more depth. While we have referenced age groups and grade levels, these are just general guidelines. For example, rather than limit the use of picture books to the youngest students, consider giving older students the chance to read aloud to younger students, so that more age/grade levels benefit. Likewise, if students find some reading selections challenging, give them an opportunity to form reading groups or partnerships.

Courage

- *Almost Astronauts: 13 Women Who Dared to Dream*, by Tanya Lee Stone; Candlewick, 2009; ages 10 and up; grade 5 and up
- *Courage & Defiance: Stories of Spies, Saboteurs, and Survivors in World War II Denmark,* by Deborah Hopkinson; Scholastic Press, 2015; ages 9 and up; grades 4 and up
- *Courage Has No Color: The True Story of the Triple Nickles, America's First Black Paratroopers,* by Tanya Lee Stone; Candlewick, 2013; ages 10 and up; grades 5 and up
- *The Boys Who Challenged Hitler,* by Phillip Hoose; Farrar, Straus and Giroux, 2015; ages 12 and up; grades 7 and up
- *Dear Mrs. Parks: A Dialogue with Today's Youth*, by Rosa Parks; Lee & Low Books, 2013; ages 10 and up; grades 5 and up
- *Eleanor, Quiet No More*, by Doreen Rappaport, illustrated by Gary Kelley; Disney-Hyperion, 2012; ages 8 and up; grades 3 and up
- *Passage to Freedom: The Sugihara Story*, by Ken Mochizuki, illustrated by Dom Lee; Lee & Low Books, 2002; ages 9 and up; grades 4 and up
- *Quiet Hero: The Ira Hayes Story*, by S.D. Nelson; Lee & Low Books, 2002; ages 9 and up; grades 4 and up
- *Rosa*, by Nikki Giovanni, illustrated by Bryan Collier; Square Fish, 2007; ages 8 and up; grades 3 and up
- *Spaghetti in a Hot Dog Bun: Having the Courage to Be Who You Are*, by Maria Dismondy, illustrated by Kimberly Shaw-Peterson; Making Spirits Bright: One Book at a Time, 2011; ages 7 and up; grades 2 and up

Determination, Meeting a Goal

- *Apples to Oregon: Being the (Slightly) True Narrative of How a Brave Pioneer Father Brought Apples, Peaches, Pears, Plums, Grapes, and Cherries (and Children) Across the Plains*, by Deborah Hopkinson, illustrated by Nancy Carpenter; Aladdin, 2008; ages 8 and up; grades 3 and up
- *As Fast As Words Could Fly*, by Pamela M. Tuck, illustrated by Eric Velasquez; Lee & Low Books, 2013; ages 8 and up; grades 3 and up
- *Enrique's Journey (The Young Adult Adaptation): The True Story of a Boy Determined to Reunite with His Mother*, by Sonia Nazario; Ember, 2014; Ages 11 and up; grades 6 and up
- *How Many Days to America?* by Eve Bunting, illustrated by Beth Peck; Houghton Mifflin Harcourt, 2015; ages 5 and up; grades K and up
- *Ice Dogs*, by Terry Lynn Johnson; HMH Books for Young Readers, 2015; Ages 10 and up; grades 5 and up
- *Little House on the Prairie*, by Laura Ingalls Wilder; Library of America, 2012; ages 10 and up; grades 5 and up
- *Oliver's Game*, by Matt Taveres; Candlewick, 2009; ages 7 and up; grades 2 and up
- *Separate Is Never Equal: Sylvia Mendez & Her Family's Fight for Desegregation*, by Duncan Tonatiuh; Harry N. Abrams, 2014; ages 7 and up; grades 2 and up
- *Snowflake Bentley*, by Jacqueline Briggs Martin, illustrated by Mary Azarian; HMH Books for Young Readers, 2009; ages 5 and up; grades K and up
- *Twenty-Two Cents: Muhammad Yunus and the Village Bank*, by Paula Yoo, illustrated by Jamel Akib; Lee & Low Books, 2014; ages 8 and up; grades 3 and up

Emotional/Social Intelligence, Cooperation

- *Cookies: Bite-Size Lessons*, by Amy Krouse Rosenthal, illustrated by Jane Dyer; HarperCollins, 2006; ages 5 and up; grades K and up
- *Conflict Resolution: When Friends Fight*, by Liz George; C. Press/F. Watts Trade, 2015; ages 7 and up; grades 2 and up
- *Diary of a 6th Grade Ninja*, by Marcus Emerson, Sal Hunter, and Noah Child; CreateSpace Independent Publishing Platform, 2013; ages 9 and up; grades 4 and up
- *Empathy: I Know How You Feel*, by Liz George; C. Press/F. Watts Trade, 2015; ages 7 and up; grades 2 and up
- *Enemy Pie*, by Derek Munson; Chronicle Books, 2000; ages 5 and up; grades K and up

- *Every Body's Talking: What We Say Without Words*, by Donna Jackson; 21st Century, 2014; ages 9 and up; grades 5 and up
- *The Feelings Book: The Care and Keeping of Your Emotions*, by Dr. Lynda Madison, illustrated by Josee Masse; American Girl, 2013; ages 9 and up; grades 4 and up
- *How to Take the Grrrr Out of Anger*, by Elizabeth Verdick and Marjorie Lisovskis; Free Spirit Publishing, 2002; ages 8 and up; grades 3 and up
- *If the World Were a Village*, by David J. Smith, illustrated by Shelagh Armstrong; Kids Can Press, 2011; ages 8 and up; grades 3 and up
- *I Just Don't Like the Sound of No!* by Julia Cook, illustrated by Kelsey De Weerd; Boys Town Press, 2011; ages 7 and up; grades 2 and up
- *Inspiring Stories of Sportsmanship*, by Brad Herzog; Free Spirit Publishing, 2014; ages 8 and up; grades 3 and up
- *A Little Peace*, by Barbara Kerley; National Geographic Children's Books, 2007; ages 6 and up; grades 1 and up
- *One,* by Kathryn Otoshi; KO Kids Books, 2008; ages 5 and up; grades K and up
- *Sorry!* by Trudy Ludwig, illustrated by Maurie J. Manning; Tricycle Press, 2006; ages 7 and up; grades 2 and up
- *The Three Questions*, based on a story by Tolstoy, by Jon J. Muth; Scholastic Press, 2002; ages 6 and up; grades 1 and up
- *We Are Citizens*, by Laine Falk; Scholastic News Nonfiction Readers, 2009; ages 7 and up; grades 2 and up
- *What If Everybody Did That?* by Ellen Javernick, illustrated by Colleen M. Madden; Two Lions, 2010; ages 7 and up; grade 2 and up
- *When Sophie's Feelings Are Really, Really Hurt*, by Molly Bang; The Blue Sky Press, 2015; ages 5 and up; grades K and up
- *When Sophie Gets Angry—Really, Really Angry*, by Molly Bang; The Blue Sky Press, 2001; ages 5 and up; grades K and up
- *When You Reach Me*, by Rebecca Stead; Yearling Newbery, 2010; ages 9 and up; grades 4 and up

Gratitude, Giving, and Generosity

- *An Awesome Book of Thanks*, by Dallas Clayton; Two Lions, 2010; ages 5 and up; grades K and up
- *Boxes for Katje*, by Candace Fleming; Farrar, Strous and Giroux, 2003; ages 5 and up; grades K and up
- *The Giving Book: Open the Door to a Lifetime of Giving*, by Ellen Sabin; Watering Can, 2004; ages 5 and up; grades K and up
- *Have You Filled a Bucket Today?: A Guide to Daily Happiness for Kids*, by Carol McCloud, illustrated by David Messing; Bucket Fillers, Inc., 2015; all ages
- *Inspiring Others (Kids Making a Difference)*, by Vic Parker; Heinemann, 2012; ages 8 and up; grades 3 and up
- *The Kid's Guide to Service Projects: Over 500 Service Ideas for Young People Who Want to Make a Difference*, by Barbara A. Lewis; Free Spirit Publishing, 2009; ages 8 and up; grades 3 and up
- *Kindness and Generosity: It Starts with Me*, by Jodie Shepherd; C. Press/F. Watts Trade, 2015; ages 7 and up; grades 2 and up
- *Mama, I'll Give You the World*, by Roni Schotter, illustrated by S. Saelig Gallagher; Dragonfly Books, 2013; ages 5 and up; grades K and up
- *Miss Rumphius*, by Barbara Cooney; Puffin Books, 1985; ages 7 and up; grades 2 and up
- *One Hen: How One Small Loan Made a Big Difference*, by Katie Smith Milway; Kids Can Press, 2009; ages 9 and up; grades 4 and up
- *Pay It Forward: Young Readers Edition*, by Catherine Ryan Hyde; Simon & Schuster, 2014; ages 9 and up; grades 4 and up
- *Thankfulness: A Gratitude Attitude*, by Liz George; C. Press/F. Watts Trade, 2015; ages 7 and up; grades 2 and up
- *Thank You, Sarah: The Woman Who Saved Thanksgiving*, by Laurie Halse Anderson; Simon & Schuster, 2005; ages 7 and up; grades 2 and up

Hard work, Conscientiousness

- *Building Our House*, by Jonathan Bean; Farrar, Strous and Giroux, 2013; ages 3 and up
- *The Curious Garden*, by Peter Brown; Little Brown Books for Young Readers, 2009; ages 5 and up; grades K and up

- *Game, Set, Match, Champion Arthur Ashe*, by Crystal Hubbard, Illustrated by Kevin Belford; Lee & Low Books, 2010; ages 8 and up; grades 3 and up
- *The Mangrove Tree: Planting Trees to Feed Families*, by Susan L. Roth and Cindy Trumbore; Lee & Low Books, 2011; ages 8 and up; grades 3 and up
- *My Story, My Dance: Robert Battle's Journey to Alvin Ailey*, by Lesa Cline-Ransome, illustrated by James E. Ransome; Simon & Schuster, 2015; ages 8 and up; grades 3 and up
- *Sally Jean, the Bicycle Queen*, by Cari Best, illustrated by Christine Davenier; Farrar, Straus and Giroux, 2006; ages 6 and up; grades 1 and up
- *See You Later, Procrastinator!* by Pamela Espeland and Elizabeth Verdick; Free Spirit Publishing, 2007; ages 8 and up; grades 3 and up
- *The Tree Lady: The True Story of How One Tree-Loving Woman Changed a City Forever*, by H. Joseph Hopkins, illustrated by Jill McElmurry; Beach Lane Books, 2013; Ages 8 and up; grades 3 and up

Mistakes, Overcoming Perfectionism

- *Beautiful Oops!* by Barney Saltzberg; Workman Publishing Company, 2010; ages 5 and up; grades K and up
- *Everybody Makes Mistakes*, by Christine Kole MacLean, illustrated by Cynthia Decker; Dutton Juvenile, 2005; ages 6 and up; grades 1 and up
- *Mistakes That Worked*, by Charlotte Jones, illustrated by John O'Brien; Delacorte Books for Young Readers, 1994; ages 9 and up; grades 4 and up
- *Nobody's Perfect: A Story for Children About Perfectionism*, by Ellen Flanagan Burns, illustrated by Erica Pelton Villnave; Magination, 2008; Ages 8 and up; grades 3 and up

Open-mindedness

- *An Awesome Book*, by Dallas Clayton; HarperCollins, 2012; ages 8 and up; grades 3 and up
- *Because of Mr. Terupt*, by Rob Buyea; Yearling Newbery, 2011; ages 9 and up; grades 4 and up
- *The Dot*, by Peter H. Reynolds; Candlewick, 2003; all ages
- *Girls Think of Everything: Stories of Ingenious Inventions by Women*, by Catherine Thimmesh, illustrated by Melissa Sweet; HMH Books for Young Readers, 2002; ages 10 and up; grades 5 and up

- *A Home for Mr. Emerson*, by Barbara Kerley, illustrated by Edwin Fotheringham; Scholastic Press, 2014; ages 9 and up; grades 4 and up
- *How We Are Smart*, by W. Nikola-Lisa, Illustrated by Sean Qualls; Lee & Low Books, 2002; ages 10 and up; grades 5 and up
- *Ish*, by Peter H. Reynolds; Candlewick, 2004; all ages
- *On a Beam of Light: A Story of Albert Einstein*, by Jennifer Berne, illustrated by Vladimir Radunsky; Chronicle Books, 2013; ages 7 and up; grades 2 and up
- *A River of Words: The Story of William Carlos Williams*, by Jen Bryant, illustrated by Melissa Sweet; Eerdmans Books for Young Readers, 2008; ages 8 and up; grades 3 and up
- *Sweet Dreams, Sahara*, by Kristiana Colón, illustrated by Luis Contreras; Tiger Stripe Publishing; ages 6 and up; grades 1 and up
- *Your Fantastic, Elastic Brain: Stretch It, Shape It*, by JoAnn Deak, Ph.D., illustrated by Sarah Ackerley; Little Pickle Press; ages 6 and up; grades 1 and up

Optimism

- *The Boy Who Harnessed the Wind: Creating Currents of Electricity and Hope*, by William Kamkwamba and Bryan Mealer; William Morrow, 2010; ages 10 and up; grades 5 and up
- *Chicken Soup for the Soul: Think Positive for Kids: 101 Stories about Good Decisions, Self-Esteem, and Positive Thinking*, by Kevin Sorbo and Amy Newmark; Chicken Soup for the Soul, 2013; ages 9 and up; grades 4 and up
- *Did I Ever Tell You How Lucky You Are?* by Dr. Seuss; Random House, 1973; ages 7 and up; grades 1 and up
- *The Gardener*, by Sarah Stewart, illustrated by David Small; Square Fish, 2007; ages 6 and up; grades 1 and up
- *Mama Crow's Gift: A Story about Family, Sharing & Optimism*, by Lory Britain; CreateSpace Independent Publishing Platform, 2011; ages 8 and up; grades 3 and up
- *Optimism: Sunny-Side Up!* by Jodie Shepherd; C. Press/F. Watts Trade, 2015; ages 7 and up; grades 2 and up

Patience, Delayed Gratification

- *If You Want to See a Whale*, by Julie Fogliano and Erin E. Stead; Roaring Brook Press, 2013; ages 7 and up; grades 2 and up

- *Lilly's Purple Plastic Purse*, by Kevin Henkes; Greenwillow Books, 2006; ages 4 and up; grades K and up
- *Waiting Is Not Easy!* by Mo Willems; Disney-Hyperion, 2014; ages 6 and up; grades 1 and up

Persistence, Perseverance

- *Almost Home,* by Joan Bauer; Puffin Books, 2013; ages 10 and up; grades 5 and up
- *The Boy Who Invented TV: The Story of Philo Farnsworth*, by Kathleen Krull, illustrated by Greg Couch; Dragonfly Books, 2014; ages 7 and up; grades 2 and up
- *The Carrot Seed*, by Ruth Krauss, illustrated by Crockett Johnson; Harper Collins, 1945; ages 5 and up; grades K and up
- *A Chair for My Mother*, by Vera B. Williams; Greenwillow Books, 2007; ages 5 and up; grades K and up
- *Hatchet*, by Gary Paulsen; Simon & Schuster, 2006; ages 10 and up; grades 5 and up
- *How to Catch a Star*, by Oliver Jeffers; Philomel Books, 2004; ages 5 and up; grades K and up
- *Ira's Shakespeare Dream*, by Glenda Armand, illustrated by Floyd Cooper; Lee & Low Books, 2015; ages 9 and up; grades 4 and up
- *Letters from Rifka*, by Karen Hesse; Square Fish, 2009; ages 9 and up; grades 4 and up
- *The Most Magnificent Thing*, by Ashley Spires; Kids Can Press, 2014; ages 6 and up; grades 1 and up
- *Out of the Ballpark*, by Alex Rodriguez, illustrated by Frank Morrison; HarperCollins 2012; ages 6 and up; grades 1 and up
- *Perseverance: I Have Grit*, by Jodie Shpherd; C. Press/F. Watts Trade, 2015; ages 7 and up; grades 2 and up
- *Ruby's Wish*, by Shirin Yim Bridges, illustrated by Sophie Blackall; Chronicle Books, 2015; ages 9 and up; grades 4 and up
- *A Wizard from the Start: The Incredible Boyhood and Amazing Inventions of Thomas Edison*, by Don Brown; HMH Books for Young Readers, 2010; ages 6 and up; grades 1 and up
- *W Is for Webster: Noah Webster and His American Dictionary*, by Tracey Fem, illustrated by Boris Kulikov; Farrar, Straus and Giroux, 2015; ages 6 and up; grades 1 and up

- *We've Got a Job: The 1963 Birmingham Children's March*, by Cynthia Levinson; Peachtree Publishers, 2015; ages 10 and up; grades 5 and up

Resilience

- *Because of Winn-Dixie*, by Kate DiCamillo; Candlewick, 2009; ages 9 and up; grades 4 and up
- *The Fantastic Flying Books of Mr. Morris Lessmore*, by William Joyce; Athenaeum Books for Young Readers, 2012; ages 8 and up; grades 3 and up
- *Finding Someplace*, by Denise Lewis Patrick; Henry Holt, 2015; ages 9 and up; grades 4 and up
- *Her Mother's Face*, by Roddy Doyle, illustrated by Freya Blackwood; Arthur A. Levine Books, 2008; ages 8 and up; grades 3 and up
- *Plunked*, by Michael Northrop; Scholastic, 2014; ages 9 and up; grades 4 and up
- *Tight Times*, by Barbara Shook Hazen, illustrated by Trina Schart Hyman; Puffin Books, 1983; ages 7 and up; grades 2 and up

Self-control, Willpower

- *The Chocolate Touch*, by Patrick Skene Catling, illustrated by Margot Apple; HarperCollins, 2006; ages 9 and up; grades 4 and up
- *My Mouth Is a Volcano!* by Julia Cook, illustrated by Carrie Hartman; National Center for Youth Issues, 2006; all ages
- *Sally Simon Simmons' Super Frustrating Day*, by Abbie Schiller, illustrated by Sam Kurtzman-Counter; The Mother Company, 2013; all ages
- *Think Before You Act: Learning About Self-Discipline and Self-Control*, by Regina Burch; Creative Teaching Press, 2002; ages 5 and up; grades K and up

Tenacity

- *Imogen's Last Stand*, by Candace Fleming, illustrated by Nancy Carpenter; Dragonfly Books, 2014; ages 6 and up; grades 1 and up
- *Turning 15 on the Road to Freedom: My Story of the Selma Voting Rights March*, by Lynda Blackmon Lowery, Elspeth Leacock and Susan Buckley, illustrated by P.J. Loughran; Dial Books, 2015; ages 12 and up; grades 7 and up
- *What Do You Stand For? For Teens: A Guide to Building Character*, by Barbara A. Lewis; Free Spirit Publishing, 2005; ages 12 and up; grades 6 and up

Poetry with Grit

- *Becoming Joe DiMaggio*, by Maria Testa; Candlewick, 2005; ages 10 and up; grades 5 and up
- *Chess Rumble*, by G. Neri, illustrated by Jesse Joshua Watson; Lee & Low Books, 2007; ages 9 and up; grades 4 and up
- *Poems to Learn by Heart,* edited by Caroline Kennedy, illustrated by Jon J. Muth; Disney-Hyperion, 2013; ages 10 and up; grades 5 and up
- *Rutherford B., Who Was He?: Poems About Presidents*, by Marilyn Singer, illustrated by John Hendrix; Disney-Hyperion, 2013; ages 9 and up; grades 4 and up
- *Swimming Upstream: Middle School Poems*, by Kristine O'Connell George; Clarion Books, 2002; ages 9 and up; grades 4 and up
- *Thank you, World*, by Alice McGinty, illustrated by Wendy Halperin; Dial, 2007; ages 8 and up; grades 3 and up
- *When Thunder Comes: Poems for Civil Rights Leaders*, by J. Patrick Lewis; Chronicle Books, 2007; ages 12 and up; grades 7 and up

Biographies

- *Abraham Lincoln for Kids: His Life and Times with 21 Activities*, by Janis Herbert; Chicago Review Press, 2007; ages 9 and up; grades 4 and up
- *Albert Einstein and Relativity for Kids: His Life and Ideas with 21 Activities and Thought Experiments*, by Jerome Pohlen; Chicago Review Press, 2012; ages 9 and up; grades 4 and up
- *Freedom Train: The Story of Harriet Tubman*, by Dorothy Sterling; Scholastic, 1987; ages 10 and up; grades 5 and up
- *Honda: The Boy Who Dreamed of Cars*, by Mark Weston, illustrated by Katie Yamasaki; Lee & Low Books, 2014; ages 8 and up; grades 3 and up
- *Helen's Big World: The Life of Helen Keller*, by Doreen Rappaport; Disney-Hyperion, 2012; ages 8 and up; grades 3 and up
- *I Am Malala: How One Girl Stood Up for Education and Changed the World (Young Readers Edition)*, by Malala Yousafzai; Little, Brown Books for Young Readers; ages 10 and up; grades 5 and up
- *I See the Crowd Roar: The Inspiring Story of William "Dummy" Hoy*, by Dr. Joseph C. Roetheli and Agnes Roetheli Gaertner; Dunham Books, 2014; ages 8 and up; grades 3 and up

- *Louis Sockalexis: Native American Baseball Pioneer*, by Bill Wise and Bill Farnsworth; Lee & Low Books, 2005; ages 7 and up; grades 2 and up
- *Milton Hershey: Young Chocolatier*, by M.M. Eboch, illustrated by Meryl Henderson; Aladdin, 2008; ages 9 and up; grades 4 and up
- *Nelson Mandela: No Easy Walk to Freedom*, by Barry Denenberg; Scholastic, 2014; ages 10 and up; grades 5 and up
- *Salt in His Shoes: Michael Jordan in Pursuit of a Dream*, by Deloris Jordan and Roslyn M. Jordan, illustrated by Kadir Nelson; Simon & Schuster Books for Young Readers, 2003; ages 8 and up; grades 3 and up
- *Sonia Sotomayor: A Tree Grows in the Bronx*, by Jonah Winter, illustrated by Edel Rodriguez; Square Fish, 2012; ages 7 and up; grades 2 and up
- *Steve Jobs: The Man Who Thought Different*, by Karen Blumenthal; Square Fish, 2012; ages 12 and up; grades 7 and up
- *Who Is Jane Goodall?* by Roberta Edwards; Grosset & Dunlap, 2012; ages 8 and up; grades 3 and up
- *Who Was Walt Disney?* by Whitney Stewart, illustrated by Nancy Harrison; Grosset & Dunlap, 2009; ages 9 and up; grades 4 and up
- *Wilma Unlimited: How Wilma Rudolph Became the World's Fastest Woman*, by Kathryn Krull, illustrated by David Diaz; HMH Books for Young Readers, 2000; ages 6 and up; grades 1 and up
- *The Wright Brothers for Kids: How They Invented the Airplane, 21 Activities Exploring the Science and History of Flight*, by Mary Kay Carson; Chicago Review Press, 2003; ages 9 and up; grades 4 and up

Notes

Chapter 1

- Duckworth, Angela L., Christopher Peterson, Michael D. Matthews, and Dennis R. Kelly. "Grit: Perseverance and Passion for Long-term Goals." *Journal of Personality and Social Psychology* 92, no. 6 (2007): 1087–101.
- Dweck, Carol. "Brainology: Transforming Students' Motivation to Learn." 2008. http://www.mindsetworks.com/websitemedia/info/brainology_intro_pres.pdf.
- Dweck, Carol S. *Mindset: The New Psychology of Success*. New York: Random House, 2007.
- Hamblin, James. "100 Percent Is Overrated." *The Atlantic*. June 30, 2015. http://www.theatlantic.com/education/archive/2015/06/the-s-word/397205/.
- Packard, E. "Grit: It's What Separates the Best from the Merely Good." *Monitor on Psychology* 38, no. 10 (2007).
- Perkins-Gough, Deborah. "The Significance of Grit: A Conversation with Angela Lee Duckworth." *Educational Leadership* 71, no. 1 (2013).
- "Promoting Grit, Tenacity, and Perseverance: Critical Factors for Success in the 21st Century." 2013. http://pgbovine.net/OET-Draft-Grit-Report-2-17-13.pdf.
- Sterner, Thomas M. *The Practicing Mind: Developing Focus and Discipline in Your Life: Master Any Skill or Challenge by Learning to Love the Process.* Novato, CA.: New World Library, 2012.
- Trei, Lisa. "New Study Yields Instructive Results on How Mindset Affects Learning." Stanford University. http://news.stanford.edu/news/2007/february7/dweck-020707.html.

Chapter 2

- Maguire, Eleanor A., Katherine Woollett, and Hugo J. Spiers. "London Taxi Drivers and Bus Drivers: A Structural MRI and Neuropsychological Analysis." *Hippocampus* 16 (2006): 1091–101.
- Ohanian, Hans C. *Einstein's Mistakes: The Human Failings of Genius.* New York: W.W. Norton & Company, 2008.

Chapter 3

- Boaler, Jo. *What's Math Got to Do with It?: How Teachers and Parents Can Transform Mathematics Learning and Inspire Success*. Revised ed. New York: Penguin Books, 2015.
- Diamond, M.C. "Brain: Response to Enrichment." *International Encyclopedia of the Social & Behavioral Sciences*, 2001, 1352–358.
- Diamond, Marian C., David Krech, and Mark R. Rosenzweig. "The Effects of an Enriched Environment on the Histology of the Rat Cerebral Cortex." *The Journal of Comparative Neurology* 123, no. 1 (1964): 111–19.
- Ginott, Haim G. *Teacher and Child: a Book for Parents and Teachers*. New York: Macmillan, 1972.
- Speisman, Rachel B., Ashok Kumar, Asha Rani, Jessica M. Pastoriza, Jamie E. Severance, Thomas C. Foster, and Brandi K. Ormerod. "Environmental Enrichment Restores Neurogenesis and Rapid Acquisition in Aged Rats." *Neurobiology of Aging* 34, no. 1, (2012): 263–74.
- "Students and Teachers." In *Hidden Brain*. NPR. Shankar Vedantam. October 13, 2015. Episode 4.

Chapter 4

- Bhargava, Hansa. "WebMD Survey: Parents Don't See Kids' Stress Signs." August 1, 2015. http://www.webmd.com/news/breaking-news/kids-and-stress/20150827/stress-survey.
- Blad, Evie. "Walton Family Foundation Invests in Research on Measuring Grit, Character." (blog) *Education Week*, September 17, 2015.
- Duckworth, A. L., and D. S. Yeager. "Measurement Matters: Assessing Personal Qualities Other Than Cognitive Ability for Educational Purposes." *Educational Researcher 44*, (2015): 237–51. http://edr.sagepub.com/content/44/4/237.full.pdf html?ijkey=hixxiPxVRpaxg&keytype=ref&siteid=spedr.
- Jensen, Eric, and LeAnn Nickelsen. *Deeper Learning: 7 Powerful Strategies for In-depth and Longer-lasting Learning*. Thousand Oaks, CA: Corwin Press, 2008.
- Lahey, Jessica. *The Gift of Failure: How the Best Parents Learn to Let Go So Their Children Can Succeed*. New York: HarperCollins, 2015.
- Miller, Andrew K. *Freedom to Fail: How Do I Foster Risk-taking and Innovation in My Classroom?* Association for Supervision & Curriculum Development, 2015.

- Richland, Lindsey E., Nate Kornell, and Liche Sean Kao. "The Pretesting Effect: Do Unsuccessful Retrieval Attempts Enhance Learning?" *Journal of Experimental Psychology: Applied* 15, no. 3 (2009): 243–57.
- Shadmehr, Reza, Maurice Smith, and John Krakauer. "Error Correction, Sensory Prediction, and Adaptation in Motor Control." *The Annual Review of Neuroscience*, 2010.
- "Stress in America: Are Teens Adopting Adults' Stress Habits?" *PsycEXTRA Dataset*, 2013.

Chapter 5

- Achtziger, Anja, Thorsten Fehr, Gabriele Oettingen, Peter M. Gollwitzer, and Brigitte Rockstroh. "Strategies of Intention Formation Are Reflected in Continuous MEG Activity." *Social Neuroscience* 4, no.1, (2009): 11–27.
- Oettingen, Gabriele. *Rethinking Positive Thinking: Inside the New Science of Motivation*. Current, 2014.
- Oettingen, Gabriele, and Peter M. Gollwitzer. "Self-regulation Strategies Improve Self-discipline in Adolescents: Benefits of Mental Contrasting and Implementation Intentions." *Educational Psychology* 31, no. 1 (2010): 17–26.

Resources

- Attention Span Report. Microsoft Canada 2015. Based on "Effectiveness of an attention-training program," M.M. Sohlberg, C.A. Mateer, 1987.
- Collins, Nick. "Sir John Gurdon, Nobel Prize Winner, Was 'too Stupid' for Science at School." *The Telegraph*, October 8, 2012.
- Emmons, Robert A. *Thanks!: How the New Science of Gratitude Can Make You Happier*. Boston: Houghton Mifflin, 2007.
- Goleman, Daniel. "Thinking and Feeling Go Hand in Hand in the Classroom." March 5, 2015. http://www.danielgoleman.info/daniel-goleman-thinking-and-feeling-go-hand-in-hand-in-the-classroom/.
- Kaufman, Scott Barry. "Why Academic Tenacity Matters." *Scientific American*. April 14, 2014. http://blogs.scientificamerican.com/beautiful-minds/why-academic-tenacity-matters/.
- Lucas, Brian, and Loran Nordgren. "People Underestimate the Value of Persistence for Creative Performance." *Journal of Personality and Social Psychology* 109, no. 2, (2015): 232–43.

- Mischel, Walter. *The Marshmallow Test: Mastering Self-control*. New York: Back Bay Books, 2015.
- Nili, Uri, Hagar Goldberg, Abraham Weizman, and Yadin Dudai. "Fear Thou Not: Activity of Frontal and Temporal Circuits in Moments of Real-Life Courage." *Neuron* 66, no. 6 (2010): 949–62.
- Nyad, Diana. *Find a Way*. New York: Knopf, 2015.
- Sharot, Tali, Alison M. Riccardi, Candace M. Raio, and Elizabeth A. Phelps. "Neural Mechanisms Mediating Optimism Bias." *Nature* 450, (2007): 102–05.
- Stumm, S. Von, B. Hell, and T. Chamorro-Premuzic. "The Hungry Mind: Intellectual Curiosity Is the Third Pillar of Academic Performance." *Perspectives on Psychological Science* 6, no. 6 (2011): 574–88.
- "Supportive Relationships and Active Skill-Building Strengthen the Foundations of Resilience: Working Paper No. 13." Center on the Developing Child at Harvard University. 2015. http://developingchild.harvard.edu/resourcecategory/working-papers/.

About the Authors

A lifelong resident of Peterborough, NH, **Jim Grant** is an internationally sought-after speaker and popular author. Fellow educators regard him as one of America's most passionate advocates for children. Jim and his wife Lillian founded Staff Development for Educators (SDE) in 1986; it is now one of the nation's leading providers of professional development training for teachers. Jim's best-known book is *If You're Riding a Horse and It Dies, Get Off!*, with over 88,000 copies in print. While he has been presenting on a wide variety of topics for over 35 years, none has been more important to him than growth mindset and grit—the subject of his latest book.

Caleb Grant speaks nationally on the power of growth mindset and grit in the workplace. His belief that perseverance, passion, self-determination, work ethic, and growth mindset are foundational to creating a productive workplace culture motivated him to co-author *Grit to Go*, his first book project. Caleb is a New Hampshire native and lives with his wife Annelise and two children in Newburyport, MA.

Joyce McGreevy's work has been published by National Geographic Learning, the Great Books Foundation, Sierra Club Books, Hampton-Brown, and many others. She also writes speeches, most recently for the Social Innovation & Global Ethics Forum in Geneva, Switzerland. A specialist in language arts support for English learners, Joyce is an avid traveler and language student who occasionally puts down her suitcase in Evanston, IL.